Native Tours

Native Tours

The Anthropology
of Travel and Tourism

Erve Chambers

University of Maryland

WAVELAND
PRESS, INC.

Prospect Heights, Illinois

For information about this book, contact:
Waveland Press, Inc.
P.O. Box 400
Prospect Heights, Illinois 60070
(847) 634-0081
www.waveland.com

Contents

Preface vii

1 From Travel to Tourism   **1**
Travel in Historical Perspective   4
The Advent of Modern Tourism   12
The Tourist as Subject   18
Case Study: Touring the American Southwest   23

2 Tourism, Society, and the Political Economy   **29**
Tourism and Economic Development   32
The Distribution of Economic Costs and Benefits   36
Tourism as Work   40
Tourism Policies and Plans   42
Transnational Dimensions of Tourism   45
The Politics of Representation   49
Social Consequences of Tourism   54
Tourism and Gender   59
Case Study: Tirol and Rural Tourism   63

3 Nature, Tourism, and the Environment   **67**
Environmental Impacts of Tourism   69
Tourism to Natural Places   73
People as Nature   79
Ecotourism   84
Case Study: Ecotourism in Belize   90

4 Tourism and Culture   **93**
Tradition, Authenticity, and Modernity   94
Tourism and Ethnicity   100

The Language of Tourism   104
Material Culture, Performance, and the Built Environment   110
Tourism in Place and Space   114
Tourism in Global and Local Perspective   118
Epilogue   121

References   125

Index   131

Preface

Persons who propose to themselves a scheme for travelling, generally do it with a view to obtain, one or more of the following ends, viz. First, to make curious collections as natural philosophers, virtuosos, or antiquarians. Secondly, to improve in painting, statuary, architecture, and music. Thirdly, to obtain the reputation of being men of virtue, and of an elegant taste. Fourthly, to acquire foreign airs, and adorn their dear persons with fine clothes and new fashions, and their conversation with new phrases. Or, fifthly, to rub off local prejudices (which is indeed the most commendable motive, though not the most prevailing) and to acquire that enlarged and impartial view of men and things, which no single country can afford.

— Josiah Tucker, *Instructions for Travellers*, 1757

Josiah Tucker's measure of the motives of eighteenth-century European travelers was written during a century in which the opportunity to travel long distances was a privilege to be enjoyed by relatively few individuals. In our time, tourism is of course a much more widespread phenomenon, and it is hard to say whether the conventions of staying put or those of traveling are the best indicator of our modern (or, if you will "postmodern") condition. In terms of scholarship, travel and tourism represent rapidly growing areas for inquiry, not only in anthropology but in many related fields as well. A decade ago, influential studies devoted to trying to understand the cultural processes associated with tourism were few indeed, while in the present it has become difficult to keep track of the amount of material becoming available. This book represents an attempt to explore the parameters of this phenomenal spurt of interest in the subject, although I must admit that the task has been daunting, and I have had to leave a lot of interesting material by the wayside.

While the major goal of this book is to review anthropological contributions to the study of tourism, I have not limited myself to the research of anthropologists. There are numerous other fields that offer insight into the human consequences of travel and tourism. I have included examples from geography, economics, history, sociology, and literary criticism, as well as from the newly emerging interdisciplinary field of tourism studies. In each case, however, I endeavor to keep my focus on tourism as a kind of *cultural* practice, in which the most telling consequences are often those that are among the least apparent. A cultural perspective can help us achieve what Josiah Tucker declared to be the most commendable of travel's objectives. It can give us insight into the ways in which our "local prejudices" influence and often distort our view of this important field of study. In this respect, scholarly disciplines are themselves subject to the influences of culture and to their customary practices. Anthropology is no exception.

To date, a large part of the contribution that anthropology has made to our understanding of tourism comes in the form of ethnographic accounts of specific tourist places and situations. Others have remarked on the strengths and limits of this approach (e.g., Crick 1989). I rely extensively on ethnographic studies in this book. On the other hand, I also point to instances in which I feel that some current anthropological approaches to the study of tourism have become problematic.

One such problem is that the ethnographic approach makes it difficult to generalize beyond specific cases. Unfortunately, this does not always discourage investigators from attempting to do so. The literature is full of examples in which anthropologists and others are not careful enough to limit their observations to the specific cases they have studied. Many at least imply that their results have much wider applicability, and not a few seem to suggest a near universality for their conclusions. We will see in this book that it can be extremely difficult to generalize tourism experiences from one case to the next or to theorize general effects from a few specific instances. For example, a particular tourism activity that is judged to be beneficial to a "host" community in one instance might be discovered to be harmful to another community. In most cases, there are both costs and benefits associated with tourism development, and how these play out in a specific community or region depends in large part on the several different factors that are introduced toward the end of this preface.

Anthropological contributions to tourism research also sometimes lack sufficient historical perspective. I mean this in two ways. First, many anthropologists still write largely in the "ethnographic present," and there is a dearth of longitudinal studies that could help us understand how tourism processes operate over the long run. This is important, for example, in trying to distinguish short-term impacts on "host" communities from longer-term impacts. A tourism development that appears to be beneficial to a local community in its initial stages can turn out to have nightmarish consequences in the long run, and the reverse is also true. One exception to this tendency to focus on the present can be found in the second edition of Valene Smith's (1989) edited volume, *Hosts and Guests: The Anthropology of Tourism*. For this edition, Smith asked her contributors to "revisit" the sites of their studies and comment on any changes that may have occurred in an interval of more than a decade. These commentaries provide some of the few observations we have pertaining to the longer-term consequences of tourism in particular communities.

In another sense, the anthropological study of tourism has also been subject to some of the same historical biases that are apparent in the field of tourism research as a whole. I refer here to the tendency to regard modern tourism as an invention of Western civilization and to trace the ancestry of tourism to the elite excursions of premodern European travelers. There is sufficient evidence to challenge both of these assumptions. In this book I point, for example, to recent studies of non-elite tourist traditions in Europe, as well as to perspectives on tourism that can be gained from the study of the travel traditions of non-Western societies. In regard to the latter, I rely primarily on scholarly work devoted to the study of Japanese tourism.

Anthropologists have tended to study tourism in faraway places. One of the discipline's greatest contributions has been to demonstrate the impacts of tourism on indigenous, marginalized, and often neglected peoples. However, this predilection for observing peoples on the basis of their cultural distinctiveness from ourselves has also served to distort the way anthropologists sometimes frame tourism as a field of study. Anthropologists have tended to view tourism as a manifestation of international and mainly unequal relationships between tourists and their "hosts." They have given much less attention to domestic tourism or to touristic exchanges among social and economic peers. For example, anthropologists have paid relatively little attention to urban tourism (e.g., Sieber 1997) and to some varieties of rural tourism where distinctions between tourist and "host" behaviors are more difficult to discern. I have endeavored to balance this perspective in this book and to range both far and near for the examples of tourism that I provide.

I am also concerned in this book with the extent to which the study of tourism has been dominated by a tendency to regard the tourist as the principal dynamic in touristic experiences. I offer a challenge to this usual focus on tourist/host relations by pointing to the ways in which tourism is mediated by persons and institutions who are neither hosts nor guests. I also argue that we too often regard the local communities and regions that receive tourists as being the passive recipients of a tourist dynamic. Anthropology probably has gone as far as any other discipline in countering this tendency, but we still have a way to go. There are numerous accounts of tourist behavior and a variety of theories to help us understand the motivations of tourists, but there is precious little in the nature of complementary theories of the equally dynamic processes of "hosting" and hospitality.

None of these provisos negate the considerable contributions that anthropology has begun to make in advancing our understanding of tourism. It is worth noting that anthropological studies of tourism have matured considerably over the past couple of decades. Nelson Graburn and Roland Moore (1994) have pointed out that, while anthropologists were overwhelmingly negative in their earlier assessments of tourism, they have presently gained a much more balanced view of the subject. Perhaps chief among the recent contributions of anthropology is a growing recognition of the social and cultural complexity of touristic encounters. Four major factors contribute to this complexity and are explored in this book.

The first of these factors relates to kinds of tourism and to the activities of tourists. In chapter 1, we will trace the origins of modern Western tourism and examine several of the theories that have been offered to explain tourist motivations and behaviors. We will explore some of the social and environmental consequences of different kinds of tourism. On occasion, we will note that there can be considerable differences in the values that tourists associate with their activities and the ways in which their presence is viewed by their "hosts."

Accordingly, a second factor contributing to the complexity of tourism can be found in the variety of communities and regions in which tourism occurs. I have tended to refer to these as "host communities," although this is not an entirely accurate label because many of the people who are most affected by tourism are not in any kind of direct hosting relationship with the people who visit their communities. The term "community" is also problematic. In this book I use the term simply to refer to places of human habitation. It is important to recognize that there is considerable variation within most communities in terms of how the costs and benefits of tourism are realized. We will see that there are important differences both between and within the kinds of communities and regions that are most frequently associated with tourism. These differences play a major role in shaping the consequences of particular touristic activities.

The third factor that I deal with in this book is the mediation of tourism by individuals, and institutions, who often stand apart from the host/guest relationship and who may not live anywhere near the places where tourism occurs. These mediators include tourism planners and promoters, travel agents and guides, government officials, investors, and representatives of the hotel and transportation industries. They are the people whose business it is to create and maintain a tourism industry by anticipating tourist needs, re-creating tourism places, and trying to imbue would-be tourists with new expectations. That their motivations are not purely economic but also cultural and ideological is an important theme of this book.

The fourth factor to play a major role in tourism encounters is that of place. Tourism occurs in a variety of places. This is a favorite subject of geography, and I have benefitted here from the observations of a number of geographers. The places where tourism occurs include but are not limited to major cities, small towns, beach resorts, environmentally fragile ecosystems, large and small islands, remote villages, and vast rural or "natural" landscapes. In each case, as we will see, the physical and cultural characteristics of a place contribute to the ways in which tourism is received and to the further consequences of its presence.

The complex nature of tourism is due to the fact that each of these major factors come into play in virtually any kind of tourism experience we can imagine. No single factor is sufficient to predict or explain the consequences of tourism for any particular instance.

Another favorite subject of tourism research has to do with the issue of *authenticity*. This is also an area in which our "local prejudices" frequently prevail. We have been taught, rightly in many instances, to abhor fakery and to value those things and relationships that we perceive to be genuine. We have also learned to respect traditions simply for their longevity, without much consideration for why and how they might be maintained. But what these terms—fake, genuine, and traditional—actually mean when it comes to tourism is not always obvious. In chapter 4 of this book I will argue for a definition of authenticity that is determined primarily by a people's ability to choose for themselves those elements of stability and change which make their lives meaningful.

I make little distinction in this book between the terms *travel* and *tourism*. Obviously, tourism is a kind of travel and, as I explain in chapter 1, modern tourism is a fairly recent phenomenon that is distinct in several respects from earlier travel traditions. But I am amused by the extent to which many people attempt to distinguish between the two terms on the basis of the "quality" of traveling experiences. More often than not, such distinctions seem to me to be heavily invested in "local prejudices" of class and privilege. There are actually several reasonable definitions of tourism. For the travel industry, tourism is usually defined by the length of time that a traveler spends away from home, regardless of whether that travel is for leisure or business purposes. In some communities that receive large numbers of visitors, a "tourist" might be anyone who was not born in the place, including long-term residents who came from somewhere else. For most scholars of the subject, tourism is most often associated with leisure activities. I will not make such a strict distinction here, noting that the exclusion of business travel and other kinds of nonleisure activities can distort our view of tourism. For the purposes of this book, tourism shall be constituted of any kind of travel activity that includes the self-conscious experience of another place.

It is almost inevitable that my approach to tourism should be influenced by the places where I have conducted my own research. It has been twelve years since I first started studying tourism in Thailand, and I have made use of this experience throughout this book. I have also offered several comments pertaining to the impact of tourism development upon the citizens of the city of Baltimore, Maryland, where I lived for some ten years.

As far as I can determine, I do not have any particular axe to grind here. I do not think that tourism is a "bad" thing or a "good" thing. I do believe that it is a pervasive influence in our lives and that we often trivialize its importance. As a rule, I do not think that one kind of tourism is superior to any other. I am not convinced that what we sometimes refer to as "mass" tourism is necessarily any worse or better than other, more individualized and intellectually self-conscious expressions of the travel experience. The tourism experiences of the wealthy and of the not so wealthy and of the virtually destitute interest me in equal measure. I do, on the other hand, feel that all forms and styles of tourism should be guided by principles of sustainable resource management, honest and fair representations of those places, and people, that are toured, and by the search for equitable distributions of tourism's benefits.

I have tried to keep in mind that tourism is something we all do, and that our interest in the subject is informed by our own experiences as much as it might be guided by more scholarly studies. If it is successful in this respect, this book should help the reader put her or his travel experiences in a new light, just as my research on the subject has changed the way I think about many of my own tourism experiences. Hopefully, our further understanding of some of the social and cultural consequences of tourism will make us all better informed and more respectful travelers.

I wish to express my appreciation to Eric Chambers and Michael Paolisso for their helpful suggestions regarding an earlier version of this book, to the anonymous reviewers for Waveland Press, and to Tom Curtin, editor for Waveland Press, for his encouragement and considerable patience.

Chapter One

From Travel to Tourism

When I travel, I normally arrive at the terminal well before my departure time. I like to take this opportunity to prepare myself for the journey, reflect upon where I have been, and entertain notions of where I am headed. If I am in some distant place, I want time to explore the terminal itself, to try the food, thumb through magazines I might not be able to read, and if I am lucky meet some fellow traveler who is willing to visit for awhile. Terminals are to my mind among the best places to confront the confluence between the universal and the particular. They are built to accommodate travelers who might not be familiar with local customs or values, and yet they invariably reflect the places of their origin. Human encounters in terminals can take on a familiarity that is rare in normal discourse among strangers. It is as though the terminal provides a space where travel becomes a common denominator and where, under the right conditions, making oneself known assumes great urgency and allows for moments of unveiled sincerity (or, paradoxically, the opportunity to disregard the "facts" of one's self and fabricate a wholly new identity).

Whether they take the form of modern metropolitan airports or dusty rural bus stops, terminals are where travelers of all kinds sort themselves out and make ready for the beginnings and endings of their personal journeys. They are places where no one really belongs, intersecting between being home and being someplace else, and as such they are monuments to the human divide between traveling and staying put. We are a restless species, sharing more in our transience with the simpler life forms, such as bacteria and viruses (which, incidentally, often travel with us), than we do with many of the more complex species to which we are the most closely related. Although human progress is often measured in terms of a people's ability to maintain habitations of increasing grandeur and stability, there is an equal case to be made for tracing the advance of our species by the tracks we make in pursuit of

1

places that are not yet where we are and that are far from where we are likely to feel settled.

Because they are ambiguous environments that are shaped to accommodate multitudes of transitions and displacements, terminals provide an intriguing imagery for two concepts that are central to our understanding of the contribution of anthropology to the study of contemporary tourism. These are the concepts of *culture* and *travel*. That these two concepts, rendered as the ordinary human experiences of touring and being toured, are greatly interdependent is a major theme of this study.

Compared to some other social science disciplines, notably economics and geography, anthropology has been slow to take an interest in tourism. Besides a few early contributions, such as Valene Smith's (1989) *Hosts and Guests: The Anthropology of Tourism*, first published in 1977, major work in the area has occurred only during the past decade. This seems surprising when we consider that tourism is so obviously amiable to cultural interpretation. As an endeavor of both international importance and profound local significance, it is one of the most culturally intimate of modern industries. As consumers, we have become accustomed to participating in numerous other major global industries without encountering or entering into a relationship with those who supply and produce the goods we enjoy. The products of these industries are rarely associated with their shifting origins. We do not buy Nike shoes because they may have been assembled in Indonesia, and rarely do we even know the origins of the fuels that run our automobiles and warm our homes. But when we tour, it is much more difficult to avoid the confluence of places and the people that inhabit them. Even the most specialized styles of tourism, such as ski vacations and weekends at the beach, invariably evoke encounters between visitors and their local "hosts." No other industry has anywhere near the potential to bring consumers and producers and their "products" into such close contact. Few other occasions of human encounter provide for so many vital moments of exchange between people of strikingly different backgrounds.

Why, then, have anthropologists only recently taken more than a passing interest in the subject? Certainly one factor is the phenomenal growth of the tourist industry. It is a subject that is becoming almost impossible to ignore. But even more critical have been transformations within the discipline of anthropology that have helped make the study of tourism more appealing. These changes have altered the way many anthropologists view the concept of culture, as well as how they practice ethnography as a major vehicle for discovering cultural processes. They have several roots, including interpretive anthropology, experiments in ethnographic representation, critical theory and the postmodern critique, some experiences in applied anthropology, and recent approaches to language theory.

This shift represents a change from an anthropology that is primarily concerned with explaining how discrete cultures determine meaningfulness to a discipline that is at least equally interested in understanding how divergent meanings collide and are reconciled in new cultural frameworks. In this sense, culture is no longer bound to place or ethnicity but is also reflective of the processes and encounters that link different places and diverse people. It is not difficult to understand how this kind of shift might encourage anthropologists to devote more attention to a subject such as tourism. So long as the idea of culture remained bound in place and time and the interest of anthropologists was focused on the discrete nature of particular "cultures," phenomena such as tourism could rarely be viewed as more than an unwelcome intrusion upon the neat categories and orderly distinctions with which anthropologists were wrestling. In the rare cases in which mentions of tourism did occur in ethnographic accounts, these comments now seem superficial and overly negative. Anthropologists simply had no place to put tourists in their studies, except as occasional intruders upon the seeming isolation of their subjects.

The link between a greater appreciation of culture as a *process* and the relevance of travel and tourism as subjects of serious anthropological inquiry is explored in intriguing detail by James Clifford (1997). Clifford's speculations are especially helpful in providing a larger context for tourism study, in that he views tourism as one manifestation of a global trend toward ever-expanding modes of human displacement. It is difficult to appreciate the often-profound ambiguities of touristic activities without taking this larger context into consideration. A Western visitor to a remote Hmong village in northern Thailand might (as I have, in my own travels) find himself or herself entranced by the sense of visiting an enduring and decidedly different, clearly mysterious place. But closer familiarity with the community provides an entirely different context to such an adventure, particularly as the visitor discovers that a fifth of the "villagers" are currently living in Canada and the United States. Consider then the possibility that the "exotically" dressed woman that the visitor just photographed only recently returned from visiting her sister in Los Angeles, where she was a tourist in her own right. The boundaries between host and guest, often expressed in terms of a variety of privileges that are normally associated with having the opportunity to travel, become blurred in this larger context of displacement, in which becoming unsettled in one way or another seems to have become commonplace.

Although Clifford is most likely correct in identifying a trend toward greater incidents of displacement in the modern world, it is also possible that scholars have tended to overstate, if not romanticize, the sedentary nature of past societies. Displacement is not necessarily a condition that is unique to modernity, and travel in one form or another has quite possibly always served as a fundamental part of the human condition. It is worth questioning why so much of our historical and archaeo-logical inquiry has emphasized settlement as the primary means of our species' adaptation and continuing development and why travel has almost always been viewed as incidental, if not antithetical, to the emer-gence of past civilizations. While the great cities and communal spaces of the past certainly do reflect ingenious responses to the problems of habitation, they also serve as monuments to travel and as repositories of the ideas and artifacts that could be gained only through countless jour-neys and visitations.

If home is truly where the heart is, it might be equally possible that travel is where the imagination has thrived. As anthropologists turn their attention to subjects such as displacement, immigration, travel, diaspora, and tourism, they are not simply exploring new ground. Rather, they are bringing back to their discipline an important corrective to an emphasis on settlement as the sine qua non of culture. We find in these more recent explorations a sense of human endeavor that is less suspicious of transience.

TRAVEL IN HISTORICAL PERSPECTIVE

For Western readers, the history of travel has been written in a largely self-congratulatory manner. According to this history, travel assumes importance primarily as a result of an emergent European rest-lessness, with roots in early religious pilgrimages and in Renaissance expeditions of trade and exploration. Travel begins to look more like tourism, with a closer association to ideals of leisure and recreation, when we consider the ideals of individual betterment that were embod-ied in such eighteenth-century phenomena as the European "Grand Tour." It takes on an entirely new significance with the rapid global expansion of the European colonial powers during the nineteenth cen-tury. While incidents such as these do provide clues to current Western attitudes and practices related to modern tourism, the assumption that they constitute a comprehensive history of travel and tourism serves only to distort our understanding of tourism as a global phenomenon.

In its most extreme (and, unfortunately, not uncommon) expres-sion, modern tourism is sometimes viewed as the consequence of a uniquely Western dynamic. Emerging from the presumably closed soci-eties of medieval times, it was the Europeans who ventured forth to "dis-cover" and ultimately tried to conquer the rest of the world. In this view, tourism is seen as a relatively late manifestation of the European pow-ers' success in establishing a presence in faraway places. It was made possible by dramatic improvements in transportation and by the increased wealth and leisure that accompanied advanced industrial development during the later stages of Western capitalism. Travel is viewed as being primarily the result of a quest for wealth and economic advantage. The explorations and conquests of the European powers are seen as having been fueled by increased demands for raw material, labor, and expanded markets for European industrial products. As a relatively new type of travel experience, modern tourism is often portrayed as a kind of nostalgic visitation of the routes and byways of Western colonial expansion. By extension, the powerful and compelling market forces that drive modern tourism are sometimes seen as a new form of economic and cultural imperialism (e.g., Nash 1996). Leisure-based tourism is usually regarded as a recent phenomenon, dependent upon the expansion of capitalist enterprise and increased leisure opportunities associated with the growth of a middle class.

So long as our view of the relationships between travel and tourism is limited to these comparatively recent Western experiences, there is some merit to such an argument. The rapid spread of a tourism economy during the past century does appear to be closely linked to Western colonial expansion and to the demands of a capitalist economic system. On the other hand, a more comprehensive view can lead us to other explanations for the advent of both travel and tourism. Mary Helms (1988) has, for example, suggested that it is the quest for knowledge rather than for wealth that underlies a human propensity for travel. Helms argues that this quest for the esoteric knowledge of other places is closely associated with elite power and remains valid through time and across cultures. She maintains that human groups have always prized and sought to obtain the spiritual and secular knowledge that lies beyond the borders of their own societies and that travel has long been valued as the means to that knowledge. Although Helms does not directly address the question of tourism, the implication of her argument suggests that elements of the touristic experience probably existed long before modern times. She notes, for example, that it is misleading to assume that the motivation for any travel experience has a single purpose (such as trade or conquest) and that it is important to consider the entire context of the journey and its multiple justifications. Her account includes numerous ethnographic examples of non-Western societies, in which travel appears to occur not only for instrumental reasons but also as an expression of individuality and a desire for freedom from social constraint—motivations that have often been linked solely to modern tourism.

Our understanding of the origins of modern tourism is limited by the kinds of information we have about the past. For example, the extensive travels of pre-Columbian Indians throughout the North American continent is most easily traced through the distribution and dispersal of their trade goods, but this kind of data leads us all too readily to emphasize trade as the primary motivation for Native American journeys. We simply lack the information that might provide us with clues to other, more elusive motives, such as curiosity or the satisfaction of exploring new places. Similarly, much of the history of Western travel has been derived from written travel accounts, and as such is reflective only of the travel conventions of a "leisured" and literate class who were closely connected to the centers of political and economic power of their time. Many of the travels on which these accounts are based were sponsored by European geographical societies and business interests that had a strong interest in the resources and potential markets of these distant places. To the extent that we let ourselves be dependent on such accounts in our search for the origins of modern tourism, we are sure to inherit a bias toward asserting that the quest for economic advantage served as the primary motivation for early travel adventures.

The history of travel has proven to be an elusive subject, but it is a topic of considerable interest to a variety of disciplines. New inquiries in such fields as leisure studies, historical geography, literary criticism, and the various social sciences, have barely begun to challenge some of the assumptions that have shaped our view of this history. At least four previously held notions regarding the development of tourism have now been opened for debate and further research. The first of these, that modern tourism has its origin in a uniquely European consciousness, has been discussed above. It would be foolish to argue that Western travel traditions have *not* contributed greatly to the shaping of modern tourism. But it seems equally implausible to assume that no other traditions of travel have existed or contributed in their own right to modern tourism. For example, Kanzaki Noritake (1992) has traced many of the characteristics associated with modern Japanese tourism to travel conventions established during Japan's Edo period (1600–1868). Most of these early travels were pilgrimages to popular shrines, although their association with leisure activity and adventure also seems well established. Noritake speculates that as many as 1 in 25 Japanese traveled to one especially popular shrine each year during the mid-Edo period. Their travel was organized by travel agents (*oshi*) who served as guides and arranged for their lodging. Noritake points out that these agents were operating at least a hundred years before Thomas Cook established the first modern travel agency in Europe. They were also instrumental in shaping one of the hallmarks of Japanese tourism—the tendency to travel and tour sights in tightly knit, regimented groups. The fondness of Japanese tourists for souvenirs and, eventually, for photographs of the places they visit is also traced to conventions established during these pilgrimages. Japanese travelers were, and to some extent still are, much more inclined than Westerners to regard themselves as representatives of their social group when they traveled. Souvenirs were a way of sharing their travel experiences with these others. Noritake also notes that the Japanese word used for *souvenir* during the Edo period was changed from characters that meant the "token of a shrine" to characters that meant "local product," reflecting the increasing secularization of travel.

Research devoted to the history of tourism remains focused on the Western experience. Accounts such as that offered by Noritake can only serve to broaden our understanding of the varieties of modern touristic experiences, particularly when we attempt to interpret the behaviors of non-Western tourists. Earlier studies of Japanese tourism have, for example, interpreted the Japanese devotion to souvenir collecting as a kind of mimicry and exaggeration of Western tourism traditions. Noritake offers convincing evidence to support the idea that these behaviors are firmly rooted in distinct Japanese traditions. Indeed, some recent trends in tourism would seem to find firmer roots in the Japanese experience than they do in European conventions of the same period. For example, Takasina Shuji (1992) has pointed out that Japanese tourists of the early Edo period traveled much lighter than their European counterparts (anticipating the modern backpacker?) and that women and children travelers actually outnumbered men. European travel would, on the other hand, remain dominated by males for centuries.

A second frequently held supposition regarding the development of modern tourism relates to associations between tourism and leisure. Much of the earlier scholarship devoted to the history of tourism justifies its focus on the Western experience with the argument that modern tourism was made possible by the increased opportunities for leisure and recreation that accompanied the growth of Western capitalism, leading to the expansion of a comparatively wealthy and leisured middle class. Before this, the argument goes, travel was usually a consequence of some instrumental need, whether that be the practical pursuits of trade and commerce, or the spiritual relief associated with pilgrimages to sacred sites. A critique of these assumptions can be mounted on two fronts. First, there is scant evidence to support the idea that opportunities for leisure have invariably increased with recent changes in social organization and economic development. To the contrary, many preindustrial peoples may actually have greater amounts of leisure time (e.g., Bodley 1976). On the other hand, what does appear to be true of the Western experience is the gradual development of a sharper distinction between occasions of leisure and work. Even in this case, however, it is not at all certain that this distinction arises solely as a result of industrialization and the development of capitalist economies. Peter Burke (1995) provides ample evidence for the emergence of distinct cultural ideals of leisure and work well before the formation of capitalist states. Burke argues that the period between the thirteenth and eighteenth centuries saw increased regulation of work habits in Western society. This in turn led to the "invention" of leisure as a distinction from labor, along with new standards as to how and when leisure should occur. Throughout this period, Burke maintains, travel and recreation became increasingly associated with new, culturally delineated periods of leisure.

The idea that tourism is principally a leisure-time activity is closely related to this discussion. Most academically based scholarship is focused almost entirely on tourism as an expression of leisure. Because of this, the association of tourism with those historical developments in Western society that encouraged a sharper distinction between work and leisure does make some sense, even if it seems quite misleading on closer examination. The tourism industry generally avoids making such a distinction, including for quite obvious reasons such categories as "business travel" and "convention tourism" as within its scope of interest. Here, distinctions between work and leisure are blurred if not disregarded. The implications of this difference in terms of arriving at a comprehensive theory of tourism have yet to be explored.

We are well reminded here of Mary Helms's cautionary note that we not fall into the trap of regarding travel (or, by extension, tourism) as having singular motives. This is particularly important when we consider that Western cultural distinctions between work and leisure have had a tendency to result in a trivialization of those activities that we assign to the category of leisure. A less sharp distinction, as we might yet discover in many non-Western societies, could provide us with important clues to the multiple uses of tourism as a modern activity. Westerners who have had the opportunity to work (rather than simply recreate) in non-Western countries sometimes find it rather disconcerting to find themselves in a setting where distinctions between work and leisure seem much more fluid and less distinct. In my own experiences of this kind, while "working" in Asia and Latin America, I have often discovered "touring" and "leisure" to be an indispensable part of taking care of "business."

The idea that travel before the development of modern Western society was purely instrumental and was undertaken solely for purposes such as trade or religious obligation is wrong. The notion that modern Western tourism is limited to activities of leisure and is therefore a trivial (that is, *useless*) pursuit is equally misleading. There is little evidence to support the idea that leisure per se provides the defining moment for the advent of modern tourism.

A third assumption that is conveyed in much of the scholarship devoted to tourism is the idea that the patterns and styles associated with touristic activities were first established by the elite members of society, and that the "masses" closely followed these patterns once they had the opportunity to tour. Again, this assumption carries with it the belief that tourism is the consequence of increased leisure and wealth. Because elites had more leisure time (an arguable position) and greater wealth, their tastes in travel and recreation set the stage for modern touristic adventures. John Towner (1996), a historical geographer, has called for a more critical examination of the relationships between tourism and social class. He has also argued that a thorough history of the development of tourism requires paying as much attention to the social and cultural conditions of tourists' ordinary, nontouristic lives (what he calls the "visitor-generating area") as to their choices of tourism styles and destinations. In other words, it is as important to pay attention to where tourists are coming from as it is to look at where they are going. In this respect, often studied European touring traditions, such as the Grand Tour and the development of expensive vacation spas, can be seen as having a close association with the elite. But Towner goes on to document the emergence of other traditions that can be attributed to Europe's working class. Such traditions are embodied, for example, in distinct styles of tourism that were apparent in mill towns in Lancaster, England, during the later part of the nineteenth century. Towner notes that entire streets of Lancaster's working class often traveled together for visits to relatively inexpensive seaside resorts. Once arrived, they recreated the social links and behavioral patterns of their communities in these new settings.

I had the opportunity to observe a similar tradition some years ago during a visit to Costa Rica. In this case, the travel group was composed solely of men who worked together in a factory in San José, the country's capital. They had pooled their resources to charter a bus for a few days' recreation at a town on the Caribbean coast. Contrary to Towner's discussion of the social structure of working-class tourism in nineteenth-century England, the intent of these Costa Rican workers seemed anything but a desire to recreate the conditions of their life at home. Rather, they seemed bent on indulging themselves in the most unseemly behavior they could manage, clearly expressing their sense of superiority over the local population (putting to rest once and for all any preconception I had that "ugly" and inconsiderate tourist behavior was the sole province of wealthy European and North American travelers). All the same, I suspect that a closer examination of this group would have revealed that many of their work relationships were in fact reproduced in this new setting.

Although the tourism styles described by Towner and myself are different, they do seem to have enough in common to suggest a distinct tradition. The practice of touring in large groups that are formed out of existing communal relationships does not seem to have precedence in elite travel of the same periods of time (except, perhaps, the touring of school groups, which is a unique tradition in its own right). Indeed, the idea of "getting away from it all" is so ingrained in elite travel that it would be hard to imagine much appreciation at all for a style of tourism that serves mainly to reproduce and reinforce everyday social relationships. It might well be that many of the touristic styles that we now regard as "mass tourism" have firmer roots in these working-class patterns than they do in travel conventions established by the upper classes. It is here that we can truly appreciate Towner's insistence that a proper history of tourism needs to pay close attention to the cultural conditions that are particular to different locales of tourist origin. For the elite European traveler of the late nineteenth century, tourism appears to have emerged as a vehicle for social distinction. It had acquired both a competitive and romantic edge, in which an individual might be judged by the extent and uniqueness of his or her journeys in the pursuit of recreation and leisure. For some working-class tourists, on the other hand, the expression of solidarity and collegiality might well have been more important than individuality in planning a vacation. This could easily be judged to be a more appropriate style of tourism where the need for cooperation, shared experience, and pooled resources contributed so much to everyday survival.

In a more immediate sense, for those of us who now belong to a large and widely diverse middle class, some aspects of both traditions will probably ring true. While we derive many ideals of tourism from a rich and predominately elite travel literature that stresses individual experience and distinction, many of the more familial and communal modes of tourism still resonate in our consciousness. In our attempts to understand both the history and the cultural significance of tourism, it might well be important to pay attention to both messages.

The fourth contestable idea regarding a history of tourism relates to the very term we use to describe it. Why do we call our subject *tourism* rather than calling it *hospitality*? Is it not true that tourism and hospitality are the two sides of the same coin? Part of the answer to why we focus so much on tourism and so little on hospitality lies in the discussion that has preceded this. There is a preference toward viewing hospitality as a stable condition upon which the dynamic of tourism somehow acts. Accordingly, there is a tendency to regard modern tourism as increasingly dictating the terms of hospitality. This is a fairly complex matter. As will be discussed in the next section of this chapter, there is some justification for considering tourism as a powerful determinant of modern social relations. This does not, however, preclude the likelihood that researchers have paid far too little attention to ways in which standards of hospitality interact with tourism and, more often than is generally recognized, help determine the shape of tourist experiences.

We need to distinguish here between hospitality as a feature of the relationships between travelers and the communities they visit (the "host/guest" relationship) and the mediation of a large and pervasive hospitality industry that has emerged in response to modern tourism. Much of the scholarship devoted to tourism carries with it at least an implicit assumption that the hospitality industry has served to replace the more traditional host/guest relationship. There is certainly some merit to this position. One hallmark of modern tourism is the extent to which it is an activity that is mediated by actors, and institutions, who are not, strictly speaking, either hosts or guests (Chambers 1997). These mediators include commercial entities, such as travel agencies, hotels, and the transportation industry. They also include government agencies that have responsibility for promoting and regulating tourism within their jurisdictions. That these agents often *act* as hosts in order to attract tourists is clear to anyone who has ever read a travel brochure. What is less clear is the extent to which such acting has actually supplanted the need for more intimate standards that govern many of the relationships that occur between tourists and the people they actually encounter during their travels. It seems more likely that the hospitality industry has simply added another dimension to the business of hosting and that a more traditional sense of hospitality has continued, although inevitably in an altered and perhaps less easy to discern fashion.

A thorough history of hospitality would be a welcome addition to our study of tourism, although it is certainly beyond the scope of this small book. One topic of interest would be to look for continuities across cultures in the ways in which hosting has been managed. Travelers' reports help us identify some of these. For example, food and drink appear to play an important role in hospitality, often being the first gesture made toward a traveler. In many societies, hospitality has been regarded as an obligation that cannot be paid for, to the extent that an attempt to compensate a host for shelter or food is regarded as a grave insult. Many societies have also included security as requisite of hospitality, with hosts assuming responsibility for the safety and well-being of their guests. Many of these roles, such as the provision of food, shelter, and security, have been assumed by the hospitality industry. This does not, however, preclude them from being acted out in other ways as a result of more personal relationships. The visitor to a place who is fortunate enough to actually form a relationship with a local is likely to find herself or himself subject to an entirely different set of conventions governing the roles of host and guest.

The persistence of noncommercialized patterns of hospitality should not surprise us. In another vein, R. C. Wood (1994) has argued that even commercialized hospitality, so closely associated with modern tourism, is not so narrowly impersonal as we might assume. Pointing out again that the study of hospitality has been neglected, Wood suggests that even the seemingly "impersonal organizational structures" of the hospitality industry yield to culturally patterned principles of reciprocity and exchange. We cannot understand these patterns if we limit ourselves to thinking of hospitality as strictly a vehicle for economic exchange and disregard the important social exchanges that persist despite the commercialization of the industry.

In this section, I have argued that there are four common suppositions concerning the advent of modern tourism that, while important in their own right, are often exaggerated to an extent that limits our understanding of the breadth of our subject. These are: (1) the assumption that modern tourism derives solely from the Western experience; (2) a tendency to associate tourism almost exclusively with leisure activity; (3) an emphasis upon the development of elite travel traditions; and (4) a neglect of the dynamics of hospitality.

THE ADVENT OF MODERN TOURISM

Any distinction between the modern age and its precedents is bound to be arbitrary, particularly as we strive for a global view of tourism. While modernity is often associated in the Western experience with the industrial age and the emergence of capitalist economies, we have noted above several ways in which attributing tourism to these late-occurring phenomena distorts our view of historical travel and tourism. It might well be that a distinctly modern tourism can only be defined by degrees and not in terms of dramatic differences in styles of travel or by drawing sharp distinctions between the motivations of tourists past or present. One such degree must certainly be found in the extent to which tourism has come to be regarded as a distinctly organized and increasingly rationalized activity. There are two important respects in which this intensification, occurring in the West toward the middle of the nineteenth century, does represent a shift toward modernity. One of these is the realization that tourism can be profitably organized and managed on a relatively large scale, thereby setting the stage for a tourism *industry* (as distinct from the practice of conventional hospitality). The other is the broadened and increasingly secularized recognition of tourism as an important means of cultural representation and affirmation. As we will see, both these shifts provide powerful rationales for the mediation of the tourism experience beyond the more traditional conventions of visitation and hospitality.

British entrepreneur Thomas Cook is often credited with having started the tourist industry. There was, however, nothing new in his offering of "package tours" during the middle of the nineteenth century, first to English resort towns and later abroad. Well before Cook's time, successful pilgrimages had required considerable skill and foresight in anticipating both the needs and interests of travelers. By the end of the eighteenth century, several other entrepreneurs had begun to offer all-inclusive excursions throughout Europe. These more secular experiences, rooted in the traditions of the Grand Tour, served to reduce the amount of effort individual travelers had to spend in planning their own holidays. They made travel easier for those who could afford it.

By the time Thomas Cook came along, the precedent for leisure group travel was well established in Europe. What Cook did add was a link to the modern and most particularly a critical association with the new economics of industrial capitalism. In this respect, Cook's unprecedented success in tourism development was very much a product of his times. It would not have been possible, for example, without the rapid innovations in transportation that were created as a result of a rapidly changing industrial economy. His package tours were built on the backs of the railroads and steamship companies that had been created to serve the needs of Europe's new manufacturing industries. Still, Cook's ultimate success depended on more than simply taking advantage of the modes of transportation that had helped fuel industrial expansion. He also helped nudge the hospitality industry into the ideology of capitalism by demonstrating that its business could be efficiently organized and managed and, given sufficient capital investment, operated on a scale never before imagined. In addition to this, and fully in the spirit of capitalistic enterprise, Cook and his followers in the new tourism industry demonstrated that the growth of tourism depended on much more than catering to the whims of travelers. It meant creating new markets for tourism, increasing the demand for travel opportunities, and in some respects even reinventing the places where tourists might be directed. The relationships between travelers and their hosts would never again be the same. Travel agencies (and later transportation companies, hotel chains, and entire governments) had begun to *mediate* tourism in ways that went far beyond the initial expectations of travelers or the particular characteristics of the places they might visit. The industry itself was beginning to create new expectations. This distinctly modern tourism industry quickly became dependent on creating demand where it had not previously existed, and on re-creating tourist locales to match these new demands.

The relationships between modern tourism and rapid industrial development were quickly established in many parts of the world. In North America, for example, the same railroads and steamship lines that carried the raw materials of industry to eastern port cities transported tourists to the regions that provided these materials. Remote parts of the country that had previously been accessible only by difficult and time-consuming stage transportation were now more easily reached, and tourist resorts began to spring up throughout the eastern United States mountain regions. Many of the early hotels and resorts that catered to tourists were actually built and managed by railroad companies, and their advertisements and promotions helped create newly desirable holiday locales in the American imagination. Rail excursions offered at least momentary relief from the strains and ills associated with rapid industrial expansion in the cities. It is ironic that, in so many instances, the same forces that drew city dwellers to the "natural" environments of the mountains served also to create less healthy and clearly unnatural situations for those who had settled these same regions before the coming of the railroads. In the Appalachian region, for example, tour companies had to go to some effort to shield the eyes of vacationers from the harsh realities of the coal mining regions they were visiting.

Such efforts to create pristine tourist environments amidst poverty and human suffering were seldom wholly successful, and they are equally problematic in our time. While we might hope that travel will open our eyes to the world and increase our understanding of the people we encounter, this is not always the most likely result. One of the reasons lies in the close relationship between modern tourism and some of the less admirable features of capitalistic economic systems that we are now considering.

In his book *Two Worlds in the Tennessee Mountains*, David Hsiung (1997) traces the origins of Appalachian stereotypes, including the "hillbilly" images that would come to dominate many American impressions of the region. He views the persistent images of backwardness, isolation, violent behaviors, and quaint ignorance as being closely related to regional conflicts that arose as a result of the struggle to build a railroad in the region during the middle of the nineteenth century. The "hillbillies" were, in effect, those who failed to appreciate the advantages of the railroad and resisted its construction as well as its implications. Hsiung points out that local railroad advocates (forward-looking citizens who were well connected with the eastern centers of industry) viewed the railroad both as a means of taking raw materials to eastern markets and of bringing visitors into the region. The tourists and other educated immigrants who might be attracted to the region would, in turn, create new and lucrative markets within Appalachia. Many of the early accounts of "hillbilly" (i.e., mountaineer) life were written by these visitors and supporters of the railroad. Hsiung argues that the mountaineers were never as unconnected from their times as these first images of them would suggest and that the writers had little real understanding of the mountaineers' society. Rather, they borrowed their images from the more progressive members of the local population. These were townspeople whose views of the mountaineers were colored by the resistance they encountered in attempting to bring "civilization" to the region. The largely negative images that are associated with mountaineer lifestyles are, in Hsiung's view, the product of local rivalries that were translated into persistent tales of "otherness" by visitors to Appalachia.

To this point, we have discussed modern tourism as a consequence of its association with capitalistic enterprise and ideology. We have noted that the advent of modern tourism is linked to the infrastructure, such as improved transportation, that helped support early industrial capitalism, as well as to the development of tourism as a capitalistic industry in its own right. While these are important factors in accounting for the unprecedented expansion of tourism in our time, they are far from adequate in providing a full explanation. Another feature of modernity that needs to be considered is its association with the sensibilities of *reason* and *rationality*. A fundamental characteristic of the modern age, inherited in part from Enlightenment ideology, is that everything of value has to have a reason and a rational explanation. Again, the difference between being "modern" or not is in this regard probably more a difference of degree than of kind. It is impossible to imagine any human society that lacks some sense of linking social actions with reason. On the other hand, in our time we do appear to have become attached to particular forms of reason-ability. We are intolerant of dogma, suspicious of the mysterious, and in large measure place our greatest confidence in those patterns of thought that are dictated by rules of presumably rational and objective scientific explanation. It is not enough, for example, that we should have laws and accept those laws on the basis of tradition or by the decree of others who are privileged to make laws without explanation. We generally expect to have reasons for our laws that are founded in an empirical way upon our understanding of human nature.

What does all this have to do with tourism? Quite a bit, actually. What we see with the emergence of modern tourism within the Western experience is a need to have more *reasons* for people to tour. What is more, these reasons have to be consistent with the beliefs and values of their time. They need to seem rational and be reflective of our scientific understanding of the human condition. Tourism, travel, and leisure cannot be ends in their own right. These things must have purposes. Here is where culturally influenced ideas of leisure and ideas of what we think we should do with our leisure seem important. While we have noted that leisure itself is not a distinct attribute of our time, the idea of highly organized leisure in the form of vacations and holidays does seem to be uniquely associated with modernity. As a cornerstone of modern tourism, the "vacation" is nothing less than organized and rationalized leisure. In other words, it is often not really leisure at all.

Again, the reasons that came to underlie modern tourism in the West have precedence in earlier rationales for travel. The religious motives that supported pilgrimages throughout Europe came, for example, to provide reasons for related kinds of travel. Many of the early beach and mountain tourist destinations in the United States were founded by church groups and served originally as retreats for parishioners who sought relief from the spiritual trials associated with competitive capitalism and industrialized urban places. This idea of tourism as a kind of *retreat* was rapidly secularized, although it has retained in many respects the notion that a tourism experience should in some respect be transformative if not vaguely sacred. For example, we still "worship" the sun, commune with nature, seek the solace of nonordinary travel experiences, and value the re-*creational* features of tourism.

One of the major reasons invented for modern tourism is that it is good for us. To appreciate the significance of this shift, we might keep in mind that the word *travel* derives from the Middle English word *travail*, which is associated with difficult, onerous, and torturous realms of experience. Modern, organized tourism opportunities offered considerable relief from the risks associated with travel, and its rationalization was dependent on convincing people that travel was not only relatively easy but also beneficial to a wide variety of people. Part of this justification derived from the spiritual values associated with pilgrimages, but the critical transformation was dependent upon broadening the scope of travel to include a greater variety of leisure opportunities. As we noted above, in the highly rationalized cultures of early industrializing societies, even leisure had to be purposeful. One of the major purposes that came to underlie modern tourism was its transformative value. The major sights and places associated with early modern tourism were those that provided some significant social and personal benefit. Spiritual benefits were provided by religious retreats and by opportunities to commune with nature. For some, intellectual benefits could be attained by participating in educational programs that were offered at popular tourist resorts. The summer educational programs offered at New York's Lake Chautauqua, beginning in 1874, provide an example of this rationale for tourism, as does the still prevalent notion of devoting part of one's vacation to catch up on one's reading. It is at this time that benefits in terms of physical health also came to be associated with tourism. People were encouraged to spend their leisure time away from the cities in which they were employed in order to enjoy the more healthy and wholesome environments of the mountains and beaches. This was, of course, well before sunbathing became associated with skin cancer and, for that matter, before the invention of the bikini. Opportunities to re-create one's physical self evolved quickly into a wealth of recreational sports and activities that continue to play a significant role in the tourism experience.

The benefits associated with modern tourism have social and economic implications as well as more personal rationalizations. In the West, early industrialization resulted in a decrease of leisure time for many laborers, and by the middle of the nineteenth century social reformers were arguing that the captains of industry could ensure themselves a more productive workforce if they granted their laborers regular opportunities for well-spent leisure. The modern paid vacation was rationalized as much as a means of increasing industrial productivity as it was intended to provide relief to those who toiled on the behalf of industry.

Modern tourism came to be imbued as well with other economic and political rationalizations. Tourism could, for example, serve the purposes of modernity by spreading "civilization" to less developed parts of the world. We have already seen how this purpose helped justify the development of railroads in Appalachia. While the major intent of the railroad was to bring raw materials to the eastern seaboard cities, the return trip could be used to bring tourists to Appalachia. Many of the tourist hotels and resorts established during this era were built by the railroads as a means of increasing their profitability and, as we noted with Hsiung's study of Appalachia, to bring sympathetic supporters of development to the regions of their expansion. From the start, there was a close association between modern tourism development and the processes of both internal and external colonialism. The first steamship companies to offer North American and European travelers opportunities to take cruises to Central America were those that were already engaged in transporting Central American bananas and other produce to cities in the United States and elsewhere.

In a similar vein, an early justification of modern tourism can be found in its relationships to nation building. For example, travelers to the southwestern United States were encouraged to indulge their interests in Native American and Hispanic cultures in association with ideals of social and political conquest. The Indian peoples of the region were interpreted for tourists not only in respect to their cultural uniqueness, but also as symbols of Western expansion. In this respect, it is worth noting that the first railroad tours of the American southwest occurred only a few years after Custer's infamous "last stand" in 1876, affording travelers with opportunities to visit safely a barely conquered people. International tourism could also serve the interests of Western nation building. The travel accounts of Western visitors to other parts of the world routinely contrasted the stage of development of modern Western nations with those of the places visited. They were, for the most part, dedicated to instilling national pride in the minds of their readers. There are notable exceptions. One need only read Mark Twain's (1897) *Following the Equator* to find one tourist's challenge to the superiority of modern Western nations.

In the West, the advent of modern tourism required both organized means of mass travel and new or rerationalized reasons for travel. It arose in close association with industrial capitalism, was furthered by entrepreneurs such as Thomas Cook, and also developed as a subsidiary enterprise by the rapidly expanding transportation industry. The idea of leisure had to be reinvented and provided with purposes that would appeal to potential tourists as well as to those who controlled the terms of their labor. Changes in the workplace associated with industrial employment contributed to the standarization of holidays and vacations. The tourism industry helped create an imagery of recreational tourism that focused on spiritual and physical well-being and deemphasized the risks and discomforts that had long been associated with travel. These factors played a major role in the way early modern tourists viewed the sights and interacted with the people of their travels.

THE TOURIST AS SUBJECT

In the preceding section, we considered those events and shifts of consciousness that helped give rise to modern tourism, at least as it has been expressed in Western culture. It seems a logical next step to ask how these general trends actually serve to motivate travel. If there is a modern tourism, then there must also be modern tourists. Who are these creatures? As soon as we begin to ask the question, we confront an array of possibilities. The image of the sunbather basking on a tropical island beach is familiar enough. A tour bus pulling up alongside the Eiffel Tower releases a load of camera-toting persons who clearly deserve to be called tourists. But what of the student visiting Japan on a study-abroad program? Or the German businessperson newly arrived in Rio de Janerio to market his goods? Where do we place a planeload of Southeast Asian refugees stepping off their airplane in Los Angeles? Or, for that matter, am I a tourist when I key my computer into the Internet and pay a "visit" to some township in South Africa?

For the tourism industry, the decision as to who is or is not a tourist is fairly simple and pragmatic. A tourist is anyone who spends a certain amount of time or travels a specified distance away from home. Tourism is tallied in the numbers of hotels rooms occupied, planes and buses filled, and meals consumed. For these purposes, my Internet travels are irrelevant—unless, of course, they motivate me to take a trip. On the other hand, the businessperson who spends a couple of nights in San Francisco and never leaves her hotel except to visit a client is every bit as much a tourist as the sightseer or sunbather.

The scholarly literature devoted to tourists is rarely so broadly focused. Here, interest lies almost exclusively with persons who are engaged in activities of discovery, leisure, and recreation. One such scholar, the sociologist Dean MacCannell (1989), has gone so far as to subtitle his book *The Tourist* as "a new theory of the leisure class." Attempts to describe tourists and explain their motivations and behaviors have generally taken one of two approaches. Contributors such as MacCannell have attempted theories that explain tourists' motivations as a consequence of their social and cultural conditioning. Others, grappling with the realization that people tour in a great variety of ways and for different reasons, have proposed typologies of tourists.

Several of the theories of tourism are centered on how tourists regard the objects of their travels. In *The Image: A Guide to Pseudo-Events in America*, Daniel Boorstin (1961) describes tourism as one of the major "pseudo-events" that have accompanied modern times. For Boorstin, modern tourism is lacking in either sophistication or insight and is representative of the tourist's readiness to accept superficiality and perhaps even to prefer fakery and contrived experiences over "genuine" travel experiences. Tourists not only accept the banal; they actually encourage it. There are elements of Boornstin's critique that do seem to ring true. Tourists have certainly been spotted driving through "Indian Country" in the American Southwest with no apparent interest in the actual Native American communities they pass through. Yet they eagerly purchase rubber tomahawks (possibly made in China) and feathered "eagle" headdresses (painted turkey feathers) in the gift shops they visit. Boornstin's analysis is reflective of a more general tendency for intellectuals to regard modern tourism as something less than genuine experience. It is difficult to read through his book without picking up a sense that tourism (as distinct from the higher quality "travels" of a more educated class) is a thing of the "masses," to be lamented because its powerful yet shallow imagery somehow diminishes us all.

The analysis of tourism provided by Boorstin has found its way into numerous more recent accounts. For example, George Ritzer and Allan Liska (1997) have argued that both modern tourism and its "post-modern" expressions are increasingly shaped by a process of "McDisneyization," in which tourists are encouraged to seek travel experiences that are merely reflections of their normally dehumanized, superficial, and inauthentic lives. For these authors, the epitome of this trend is "cyber-travel," in which stay-at-home tourists are free to roam the world without having to experience any of the discomforts or other realities that are associated with real travel.

MacCannell (1989) has taken a different approach. He views modern tourists as seeking to escape rather than replicate the alienated, inauthentic associations of their everyday existence. The aim of the tourist, he asserts, is to find something authentic in a world that has become increasingly disconnected and unmanageable. The idea of modernity and particularly its link to capitalistic modes of production is very much a part of MacCannell's analysis. The tourist's journey is a kind of nostalgic flight from the implications of modern life, based on a premise that life was more "real" before the emergence of industrial capitalism. The foundation for this authenticity was the connectedness people felt in their social environments—the lack of contradictions between such elements as work, family, and community.

But the modern tourist's journey to authenticity is not always easy, or even entirely possible. MacCannell does not argue that many of the sights and performances that are "staged" for tourists are authentic in their own right. Rather, he suggests that the tourists' goal is to get behind the stage that is provided for them and find something real to experience. An analogy with many people's fascination with movie actors can help explain this process. While many of us enjoy the performances of actors, we seem as a culture to be unable to accept them simply in relation to the roles they perform on screen. We want to know what they are *really* like, and a whole other industry has developed to keep us informed of the most intimate details of their real lives. MacCannell suggests that we behave in the same way as tourists. We look for sights that reflect a sense of authenticity that we feel is normally beyond our grasp.

MacCannell's analysis is consistent with some of the components of modern tourism that we considered in the preceding section of this book. In his view, modernity produces feelings of alienation and inauthenticity. But it also produces the longing for an escape to something that is real. In other words, as we noted earlier, the advent of modern tourism requires not only the *means* to tour but also culturally significant *reasons* for touring. What the tourist seeks is a kind of transcendence from the pervasive influence of *modern* life. The experience, he asserts, is not unlike a religious experience—in fact, for MacCannell "tourist attractions are precisely analogous to the religious symbolism of primitive people."

Some other scholars have conceptualized tourism even more distinctly in its relationship to sacred and quasi-sacred realms of experience, often stressing the implications of the secularization of religious pilgrimages (e.g., Graburn 1983). Many of the these approaches borrow from Victor Turner and Edith Turner's (1978) study of Christian pilgrimages and from Victor Turner's (1969) more general analysis of ritual processes. One of the unique aspects of this orientation is that it can be used to focus as much on social interactions between tourists as on the relationships of tourists to the human subjects of their travels. Following the Turners, tourism is here viewed as a process of "sacrilization," or a rite of passage, and it is authentic in its own right. Three experiences associated with sacrilization are particularly important. First, tourism, like earlier pilgrimages, results in social and spatial separation from the tourist's normal residence and social environment. This leads, secondly, to an experience of *liminality*, in which the tourist is out of normal time and place and familiar social conventions are suspended. This liminality might extend to others involved in the tourist experience. Tourist places (recall the travel terminals I alluded to at the beginning of this chapter) are often unique spaces in which "hosts" as well as travelers can become separated from normal social expectations. The third step in the process of sacrilization is a distinct bonding of tourists, or of tourists and their hosts, along the idea of Turner's concept of *communitas*. Through this stage of the process, the tourist enters into a "sacred" realm of community with others. Unlike our usual regard for community, which we tend to take for granted, the power of communitas resides in the notion that it is the result of interactions between strangers, who are active agents in its creation. Thereby, tourism becomes an opportunity for re-creation and renewal.

One impression to be gained from considering the theories of tourism discussed above should be an appreciation for how difficult, and perhaps impossible, it is to account for such a complex phenomenon as tourism on the basis of a single theoretical perspective. We can certainly find in our own experiences plenty of instances of tourist behavior that would seem to support Boorstin's and Ritzer and Liska's unflattering analyses. On the other hand, it is not hard to find other instances that would be more understandable in the terms of MacCannell's, or the Turner's, or Graburn's approaches.

Other scholars have been attentive to fact that people seem to tour for a great variety of reasons and often in strikingly different ways. They have attempted to describe tourism by differentiating kinds of tourists. For example, Valene Smith (1989) provides a typology that distinguishes modern tourists primarily on the basis of their numbers and their willingness or ability to adapt to local community norms. Smith's seven types range from the "Explorer," who is motivated by a quest for discovery and travels alone or in small groups, to the "Charter" tourist, who tours in the largest groups and seems to have considerably less desire to understand much about the places he or she visits. Tourists on the high end of Smith's typology (the Explorer, the Elite, the Offbeat, and the Unusual tourist) tend to adapt well, or least fairly well, to the local norms of the people the visit. On the lower end of the typology (the Incipient Mass, Mass, and Charter tourist), individuals adapt less well and tend to seek experiences that will keep them close in touch with the kinds of Western amenities to which they are accustomed.

Smith proceeds to a consideration of the impact that these different tourist types have on the communities they visit. Not too surprisingly, considering the way she initially describes each of the types, Smith views the high-end tourists as having the fewest impacts, and the low-end tourists as being least favorably regarded by their local hosts. Unfortunately, Smith's analysis is brief and it is difficult to judge how she actually arrived at a sense of how local populations might regard the tourists in their midst. Certainly the numbers of tourists visiting a place and the attitudes they express toward the local communities they visit are bound to have an impact of some kind or another. It is not at all certain, however, that these impacts can be as neatly associated with tourist types as Smith indicates. I am reminded of a colleague, an anthropologist who has studied tourism among the Australian Aborigines, who once suggested to me a quite different outcome. She noted that the Aborigines she visited greatly favored mass tourists because they came all at one time, got off their buses, bought a lot of things, and then got back on their buses and left the Aborigines in peace. Much more disturbing were the tourists who wanted to get a closer look at Aborigine society, who asked a lot of questions, and perhaps even wanted to live with the Aborigines for awhile. They were a real nuisance.

It will be important, particularly as we begin to consider some of the impacts of tourism on local populations, to keep in mind that what makes sense to us on the basis of our own preferences for different tourism styles might not always make the same sense to those who are visited by tourists. In this case, we certainly can appreciate the motives and goodwill of adventuresome tourists who want to become more closely involved with the people they visit. It can be disarming to discover that some tourist "hosts" might be more content just to have the tourists' money and be rid of them.

The creation of tourist types varies in relation to what features of tourism are deemed to be significant for any particular analysis. For Smith, the numbers of tourists involved and their relative adaptability to local norms are critical factors. On the other hand, John Urry's (1992) interest in tourism is primarily associated with the ways in which tourists "gaze" upon the objects of their travels. To this end, Urry has proposed five ideal types of gazing. The "romantic" tourist, for example, has a solitary vision that involves sustained immersion in a tourist place and that seeks experiences of vision and awe. The "spectaterial" tourist tends to engage in communal activities with other tourists, which are composed of brief encounters involving glancing at sights and collecting different "signs" of their travel experience. Urry's three other tourist types are the "collective," the "environmental," and "the anthropological." Urry's analysis allows for significantly different approaches to the idea of touring places.

The typologies mentioned above are *etic*, which is to say that they derive from distinctions that scholars have made to explain particular aspects of tourism. Relatively little attention has been paid to the *emic* categorizations that are made by the members of communities that receive tourists. There are a few studies that have offered such distinctions in relation to particular tourism locals. For example, Tamara Kohn (1997) has described four tourist types identified by locals on an island of the Inner Hebrides. These range from "day-trippers" to "summer-home people." Jacqueline Waldren (1997) has discussed how the categorizations of tourists made by locals on the Spanish island of Mallorca have changed over time, in response to differing political circumstances. Both these studies indicate that the category "tourist" can be fairly broad and flexible from the perspective of local residents. For example, people who are from elsewhere but have established residence in an area might still be regarded as tourists by those who have deeper roots in that place.

Even this brief discussion of theories of tourism and types of tourists should serve to increase our appreciation of the complexity of our field of study. Still, we need to keep in mind that attempts to understand tourism solely on the basis of the motives and behaviors of tourists, or in terms of the ideologies that might inform tourist motives and behaviors, is certain to leave us with only a partial appreciation for what tourism has come to represent in our time. Too often, portrayals such as these leave the impression that it is the tourist, and the production and modification of the tourist experience through a variety of mediators, that provides the dynamic that underlies tourism. The local populations that receive tourists are all too often left to play a passive role in process, as the recipients of the largess provided them by tourists or as the victims of tourism. There is perhaps no other aspect of tourism study that is so needful of correction or to which anthropology, with its close attention to locale, potentially has so much to contribute.

CASE STUDY: TOURING THE AMERICAN SOUTHWEST

The distinct landscapes and people of the American Southwest have captured the imaginations of travelers from the beginning of their "discovery" by Europeans. It was from these vast spaces, in the middle of the sixteenth century, that Cabeza de Vaca reported upon the rumored Seven Cities of Cibola, conveying the image of magnificent pueblo structures and immense riches to be had for the taking. Don Garciá López de Cárdenas's subsequent description of the Grand Canyon was scarcely believable to Europeans. Not unlike modern-day tourists, the early explorers were sometimes as careful to make note of the more ordinary aspects of their travels as they were to remark upon the spectacular, and their accounts sometimes read like modern travel guides. Upon visiting the Zuni pueblo in 1540, Francisco Vasquez de Coronado remarked that the Indians there made the "best tortillas that I have ever seen anywhere."

Places like the southwestern United States still occupy a special place in the imaginations of many people. In many respects, the imagery of the American West remains closely tied to its exploration and subsequent settlement. Less than 200 years ago, much of the Southwest was still uncharted foreign territory for citizens of the United States. On their trek across the continent during the first decade of the nineteenth century, Lewis and Clark had to beware of the risk of being apprehended by the Spanish, who still controlled much of the region. Although the Western territories attracted their share of travelers and adventurers after Lewis and Clark, the development of large-scale, organized tourism was not possible without a reliable means of providing for transportation and hospitality. These came hand in hand with the railways, barely 80 years after Lewis and Clark's journey. Determined to link the two coasts of the United States and to further the country's early industrial expansion, the railroad companies simultaneously realized the potential for tourism development along their right-of-ways. This was rarely in greater evidence than it was in the Southwest, where the first and most notable tourist facilities typically were financed and controlled by the railways.

The opening of the Southwest to tourism was accomplished largely by the Atchison, Topeka and Santa Fe Railroad, and by a hotelier named Fred Harvey, who worked as a partner with the railway in providing travelers with meals, hotels, and ultimately with much of their experience of the "authentic," still slightly wild West. The Santa Fe railroad actively promoted tours of the Southwest, directing their advertisements to wealthier families in the eastern United States. Their promotions emphasized the uniqueness of the landscape, including features like the Grand Canyon and the Petrified Forest, as well as the opportunity to see genuine Indians in their "natural" habitats, and to purchase the arts and crafts of native artisans. The railroad also sponsored trips to the Southwest for popular writers and intellectuals, who returned home to produce articles that helped rationalize travel to the region as a properly modern and transformational experience. One such writer, Harriet Moore, writing for the *Atlantic Monthly* in 1902, found Arizona to be a suitable place for a visitor to commune with nature and measure "the stature of his soul with God."

For his part, Harvey stood ready to provide tourists with the kinds of experiences that the railroad pamphleteers had promised. His hotels, in places like Albuquerque and on the rim of the Grand Canyon, brought representations of Indian culture to the tourists. Indian artisans were organized to provide their goods for sale on a platform across from Albuquerque's Alvarado Hotel. Inside the hotel, demonstrations of weaving, pottery, and silverwork were provided. Encouraging tourists to collect the artifacts of native craftsmanship found much of its rationale in Fred Harvey's own extensive collections. Many of his hotels included museum rooms, and the Alvarado Hotel provided a separate Indian Museum to house part of Harvey's collections.

The railroads' control of southwestern tourism began to decline after World War I, with the increased availability of automobiles. Fred Harvey adapted to this new trend by promoting "Indian Detours." These were road trips that promised to bring tourists from the staged authenticity of the hotels and museums to authentic Indian and Hispanic places. The popular Indian Detours added new cultural icons to the mystique of the Southwest—places like Taos Pueblo and Mesa Verde and people like the Hopi and Navajo—began to be etched in the American imagination. It is worth noting that, in addition to the recreational and sightseeing aspects of these ventures, there was also an unambiguous nationalistic spirit behind much of the promotion and staging of the tours. The early railroad excursions explicitly offered Anglo Americans the opportunity to come and visit this unique part of their now conquered country.

In many respects, Fred Harvey was America's answer to England's Thomas Cook. His genius was in organizing people and places into representations that appealed to modern tourists, and he helped encourage increasing numbers of people to begin to think of themselves as tourists. The Santa Fe/Harvey partnership contributed to the creation of a Southwest that was worth the still considerable trouble of visiting the region. In their portrayals of the cultural and natural distinctiveness of the area, which in many cases emphasized its timeless and decidedly not modern character, the railroad and its hotelier offered the opportunity for even the casual tourist to be moved, and perhaps even transformed, by his or her experience.

The opening of the southwestern United States to mass tourism provides several interesting examples of the relationships between tourism and expressions of gender (which we will discuss in greater detail in chapter 2 of this book). Women played multiple roles in the staging and accommodation of tourism in the region. Early on, the Fred Harvey Company brought young women from the East to serve in its hotels and restaurants. These "Harvey Girls" came to represent the taming of the Southwest, in that they served as models of virtuous, civilized, and Anglo-American womanhood. Every effort was made to distinguish the Harvey Girls in manner and dress from two other prominent female representations of the region—the Native American women and the prostitutes who had become a significant feature of the frontier.

Women also played prominent roles in the actual staging of southwestern tourism (Weigle 1992). Mary Colter, a designer and art teacher from Minnesota, worked with the Fred Harvey Company and the Santa Fe Railway as a principal architect of the interiors of many of their tourist facilities. Erna Fergusson, a native of New Mexico, was the first to recognize the importance of the automobile and to organize auto tours of Indian pueblos. She was later hired by the Fred Harvey Company to organize their Indian Detours. The auto tours, which began in the 1920s, mark a major transition in the way Anglo women were represented in the region's tourism industry. By this time, a thriving art colony had been built up in places like Albuquerque and Santa Fe. The Anglo women that Fergusson employed as tour guides represented the bohemian spirit of the art colonies and stood in sharp contrast to the rather staid and closely chaperoned Harvey Girls. Among other things, the women tour guides were encouraged to blend themselves into the cultural landscape by adopting variations of local, western dress.

Considerably fewer opportunities to adapt to the times were afforded to other major female participants in southwestern tourism, particularly the Indian women who had become so much a part of the tourist gaze. These women were instead transformed into symbols of southwestern traditions that, for the purposes of tourism, needed to stay the same in order to represent authenticity. Barbara Babcock (1994) has suggested that Indian women came to serve as "cultural bodies" for the touristic impulses of Anglo visitors. She has explored the representation of Indian women throughout the history of southwestern tourism, and she has paid particular attention to the enduring symbolization of Native American women in traditional dress and in close association with pottery. In this association, she asserts that Indian women and their pots serve as enduring "containers" of Anglo cultural desires. The pictorial representation of traditionally dressed Indian women with pots on their heads has remained a constant in the tourist representation the Southwest, even though, as Babcock notes, by as early as the 1920s few Pueblo women actually appeared in such a way unless they were paid to do so.

Many of the anthropological studies of the impacts of tourism that will be discussed in subsequent chapters of this book are focused on communities and regions that have only recently begun to experience tourist activity. This is not true of places like the American Southwest, where many Indian communities have now acquired several generations of experience with tourists. While there is clear evidence that many Indians bristle over the ways in which they are represented and misrepresented through tourism, there is also a growing literature that describes how many communities have adapted to the industry. Dierdre Evans-Pritchard (1989) has noted, for example, that many of the Indian communities of the Southwest have much more experience in dealing with tourists than most tourists have in dealing with Indians, and this often puts visitors at considerable disadvantage. Jill Sweet (1991) has described the ways in which some Pueblo Indian communities have managed to control and regulate their relationships with tourists. She attributes this ability to, among other things, the relatively gradual development of tourism to the region and the considerable amount of self-determination enjoyed by many Pueblo peoples.

One of the major sources of resentment on the part of some southwestern Indian communities lies in the extent to which they perceive outside merchants and other tourism mediators to be capitalizing on Native American culture for their benefit. In her study of the impact of tourism in the Taos Pueblo, a popular tourist site north of Santa Fe, New Mexico, Carol Chiago Lujan (1993) notes that community members are mostly positive in their assessment of tourism. It brings them economic gain, and many community members see tourism as reinforcing rather than eroding their cultural identity—in part because their interactions with tourists tend to leave them with a sense of the superiority of their own culture. On the other hand, Lujan noted considerable tension between the Taos Pueblo and the nearby town of Taos, whose tourism industry benefits considerably from their proximity to the Pueblo. Sylvia Rodriguez (1998), a native of the Taos Pueblo now turned anthropologist, has described the ways in which Taos Pueblo festivals serve both to accommodate tourists and to provide avenues for resisting and competing with the town of Taos for tourism's largesse.

This case study illustrates a number of points made in the chapter. The opening of the southwestern United States to tourism was closely associated with the growth of industrial capitalism, most particularly with the spread of rail transport. We have noted the extent to which tourism to this region both reflected and helped create new rationales for travel and new images for sightseeing. This case is also useful in demonstrating how difficult it can be to generalize the impacts of tourism from one locale to another. We have learned, for example, that Pueblo Indian communities enjoyed a fairly gradual introduction to tourism. They have also had quite a bit of autonomy in deciding how to handle tourists. As we will see, there are many other places where people do not have these clear advantages.

On a recent visit to Grand Canyon, I was impressed by the extent to which much of the early development of tourism to this region has now been incorporated into the actual staging of the tourist experience. Exhibits have been designed to inform visitors of the ways in which individuals like Fred Harvey and Mary Colter contributed to the design and ambience of the resort. A "Fred Harvey Company" logo, obviously of recent invention, has become a tourist icon in its own right. It appears on T-shirts and caps and other tourist paraphernalia. Fred Harvey, entrepreneur of tourism, has been transformed into a tourist object. I think this is intriguing. Are we coming to a point in which we travel to see tourism? Modern tourism now has a history of its own and with that the capacity to capture our attention—it is beginning to become a part of its own gaze.

Chapter Two

Tourism, Society, and the Political Economy

There are few places I have visited that I have not enjoyed in one way or another. I even like Disney World. When I lived in Florida, not far from Orlando, family members and friends who visited me there usually wanted me to take them to Disney World. As a result, I have learned that some people like the place and others do not. Almost everyone hates the lines. Some people also feel that it is too superficial and sanitized to be very interesting, and others do not like the considerable amount of control that is exerted over both the paying guests and Disney employees. You cannot really stroll aimlessly through Disney World. It is as though every step you take was anticipated by someone else. Still, I have come to like Disney World. I am content to suspend belief as I wait in line with hundreds of other citizens to board a pretend boat and then pass through "It's a Small World." I know that the child dolls that sing with such mechanical sweetness as I float by have no feelings or emotions, and they represent no reality I am ever going to experience. The thing is I like silly things.

Disney World is a somewhat extreme example of the mediation of tourist experiences. There is practically nothing going on there that has not been carefully planned. There is nothing that is likely to be particularly controversial or offensive to reasonably normal people. That is, of course, why some people do not like the place. On the other hand, a lot of other people keep coming back and back.

Another thing that interests me about Disney World is that most of my "hosts" there are plastic, which means that I and other visitors can do them little harm. That does not suggest, however, that visitors are not also engaged with and by real people. It just means that the individuals who are most responsible for our experience are invisible to us. They are the mediators who are hard at work trying to make sure that we feel good while we play with their toys. And toys are what Disney World is all about. Much of the genius of the place is that it provides a safe and relatively unembarassing environment for kids of all ages to engage in acts of pretense, some of which really are quite silly.

The companion of control is manipulation. There is admittedly a somewhat heavier side to places like Disney World. Stephen Fjellman (1992) has, for example, described some of the more subtle ways the theme park celebrates corporate America and excludes recognition of the unpleasant realities that have accompanied the growth of capitalism. Sharon Zukin (1991) cites the Disney enterprise as an example of a new "culture of consumption," in which visitors are enticed into thinking of consuming the world's things and images as a necessary condition of participation in modern society. Some scholars see places like Disney World as a harbinger for the future of tourism—a future that disconnects us from reality and that is bereft of sincere human contact. Personally, I doubt that is true. We read too much into the place when we try make it represent so much. After all, for all the glitz and high-tech entertainment, Disney World is just another amusement park.

Our study of tourism is incomplete if we limit ourselves to trying to understand the relationships that occur between visitors and their hosts or between tourists and the locales where they tour. On almost every level imaginable, tourism is a highly *mediated* activity. It is mediated by representatives of an industry that is among the largest in the world—ranging from government officials, tourism planners, advertising and marketing agencies, associated "hospitality" industries such as the hotel and transportation industries, travel agents and guides, travel writers and publishers, preservationists, and even by people who study tourism. Neither hosts nor guests in any tangible way, these individuals and agencies play important roles in determining where tourists go as well as what they see and do when they arrive at their destinations.

In the previous chapter, we were primarily concerned with discussing the advent of modern tourism and exploring some of the reasons for the astounding growth of the industry. Now we will begin to consider ways in which the processes that encourage tourism have helped shape the world in which we all live. To do this, we need to keep in mind that there are three important sets of actors in this process—the tourists themselves, the local people who inhabit the places that tourists visit, and the mediators who play such a great role in structuring the tourism experience. For those who serve as its mediators, tourism is generally regarded as a resource that can convey benefits to the businesses and communities that facilitate its practice. The most obvious of these benefits is wealth. Tourism has come to play a major part in the economic development schemes of places throughout the world. In many developed countries, tourism income has provided an important rationale for the revitalization of urban places and as a means to stem economic decline in rural areas. Tourism has become so popular a tool for economic development that we cannot help but wonder if there will be enough tourists to fill all the places that have been made available. The answer is clearly that there are not enough tourists to go around. This makes tourism development a highly competitive industry and a risky investment. There are important social and cultural implications associated with this competition. In the lingo of the industry, tourism's products are *destinations*. These destinations are made up of places and the people that inhabit them. Competition in the tourism industry intensifies the transformation of places into destinations that other people would like to visit. A place that once existed primarily to serve local interests now comes to be reenvisioned in ways that are intended to serve the interests and desires of outsiders. In some cases, local and visitor uses of a place might be fairly compatible. In other instances, they clearly are not.

But tourism is not only about economic gain, or about the social and cultural transformations that might occur as a direct result of this kind of economic development. It is also about the uses of power and about the ways people choose to represent themselves. In this sense, tourism has the capacity to strike at the heart of human identity. The struggle to make a tourist place includes the task of defining that place in human terms. Destinations need to have a special character in order to differentiate themselves from competing destinations. In this sense, tourism becomes a process by which interested parties have an opportunity to determine how they—their community, their city, their nation—will be represented to the rest of the world. In the end, this process has the potential to change the way people and communities think about themselves. This is an important feature of tourism development, because it fosters competition at another level. Tourism has the capability of giving rise to situations in which different segments of a community or society compete among themselves for the power and authority to determine the ways in which their places are to be represented. In some instances, this struggle may actually be more important than the hoped-for economic gains. This helps explain, for example, why some cities are willing to invest large sums of money to attract major league sports teams, even in cases in which the economic benefits of such a strategy are not at all clear.

These observations add an important wrinkle to our study of tourism. Note that most of the theories of tourism discussed in the previous chapter focus on the ways in which tourism desires and motivations help shape the tourism experience. Now we are shifting attention to the ways in which tourism's "hosts" and their mediators contribute to this same process. In this respect, we will see that tourism provides the opportunity for different segments of a community or society to compete for the opportunity to imbue places and events with identities that best represent their particular interests and values.

Tourism is a high-stakes enterprise. While it can be regarded as an industry, it does not work like most other industries that might come to mind. There are no factories, for example, and the ownership of the resources associated with tourism is often contestable. The product of tourism is experience. That is something that cannot be made uniform in the way manufactured items are made uniform. The Disney people discovered this when they built new theme parks in Japan and France and discovered that even Mickey Mouse is not culturally universal. The question of who has the right to "make" tourism is hotly contested and seldom settled. And, as I have noted, tourism is much more culturally intimate than nearly any other industry. Its business is to bring into close contact people of widely different means, class, ethnicity, and religious and cultural backgrounds.

TOURISM AND ECONOMIC DEVELOPMENT

One of the perennial problems associated with tourism development is whether, in any particular case, it makes good economic sense. To understand why this is problematic, we need to review some of the economic criteria by which tourism development is commonly evaluated. In a relatively short period of time, beginning with the end of World War II, tourism has become a significant if not vital part of the economic development strategies of most regions of the world, including the highly industrialized nations of Europe, the United States, and Japan. "Third World" and developing countries have become increasingly attracted to international tourism for its contribution to favorable foreign exchange, which is important in part as a way for many of these countries to meet their obligations of foreign debt. Within nations, some ethnic minorities have in their own right begun to view tourism as a means of creating new employment possibilities and economic opportunities for their people.

The economic criteria that are used to measure the costs and benefits of tourism are important because economic development is almost invariably put forth as the most important reason for considering tourism development. This is true even in cases where other social and cultural objectives, such as those discussed above, might actually be equally or even more significant. The reason for this is simple enough. It is far less risky and more politic for tourism advocates to argue that a particular tourism development scheme will benefit a region economically than it is to suggest that there are also important and contestable ideological and cultural reasons to proceed with the project. Unfortunately, there has been a tendency for the economic analysis of the costs and benefits of tourism to disregard social and cultural variables, in part because they are difficult to measure in conventional economic terms. There is also considerable disagreement, even among economists, as to the true meanings and reliability of some of the indicators they use to measure tourism development.

One important economic criterion associated with tourism development has to do with the *repatrition of profits*, or "leakage." This refers to the amount of economic gain from an activity that is likely leave the region or country where the goods (in this case, tourism) are produced. A considerable amount of the leakage associated with tourism results from foreign investment in the tourism development of other countries. Investors expect profit, and that profit usually returns to their countries. Foreign investment in tourism might include ownership of airlines and other transport systems, as well as ownership of hotels and entertainment and recreation facilities. Other sources of leakage include the employment of foreigners in a country's tourism industry and the necessity of importing goods to satisfy tourist demands. These goods range from building materials, vehicles and petroleum products, and various kinds of foods and spirits that are not locally produced.

The amount of profits that leak from a country or region depends greatly on the degree to which tourism investment is or is not dominated by foreign capital. It is also related to the type of tourism that is common to a region. For example, "first-class" tourist facilities often require the importation of goods that tourists expect as a part of the high cost of their accommodations. On the other hand, "low-end" or "backpacker" tourism is more likely to rely on locally produced goods and services, resulting in less leakage. In some countries that rely heavily on foreign capital investment and cater almost exclusively to first-class tourists, as much as 90 percent of the profits from tourism might leave the country. Other countries have been more successful in retaining tourism profits, generally by placing curbs on foreign investment and restricting foreign employment in the tourism sector and increasingly by encouraging "appropriate" or "sustainable" tourism developments that rely more upon locally produced goods and services.

The leakage of tourism profits across national boundaries is a particularly significant problem in developing countries that do not have the facilities or means to produce the kinds of goods required by many visitors. Still, even in places where a substantial part of the profit from tourism stays in the country, there can be questions as to how much the local population actually benefits from the industry. These questions have to do with the distribution of tourism profits within a country or region. It is clear that a large share of tourism's profits usually goes to the upper segments of society—to the people who have, in their own right, the capital to invest in tourism development. But how are the rest of the economic benefits distributed throughout a region? Economists often use the concept of the *multiplier effect* to describe the ways in which profits might be increased and redistributed among the general population of an area. These "multipliers" might, for example, include increased opportunities for wage employment, or the possibility of additional small-scale entrepreneurial activities associated with tourism, or the amount of economic benefit to be realized as a result of the domestic spending of those locals who are directly employed in the industry. Through these kinds of redistributions, the actual value of tourist expenditures might be increased by several times.

In some respects, the concept of multipliers is similar to what has sometimes been referred to as "trickle-down economics." The spirit of this approach to economic development is often to favor large capital investments that initially provide the greatest benefits to a few wealthy investors, on the assumption that additional economic benefits will trickle down to the wider community in the form of increased employment, higher wages, and improved infrastructure. Critics of the use of multipliers in tourism planning have noted that such measures tend to oversimplify the relationships between tourist expenditures and economic benefits such as employment.

Tourism development can also be evaluated in relation to its *opportunity costs*. These are the costs that are associated with participation in an industry, in respect to other kinds of opportunities that are foregone as a result. For example, if an entrepreneur decides to invest his or her time and money in a new tourist business, that means she or he has less time and money to invest elsewhere. Local governments invest in tourism by such means as offering tax incentives to investors, providing and maintaining infrastructure, and supporting efforts to promote and market tourism. Since governments have limited amounts of time and money, investment in the tourism sector can detract from opportunities to invest in other areas, such as encouraging other kinds of development or devoting more resources to public education or to the maintenance of neighborhood recreational facilities.

Tourism development can also lead to additional economic costs. For example, while a local community might profit from tourism as a direct result of increased opportunities for wage employment or entrepreneurial activities, these benefits might be offset in part by new costs, such as a rise in the prices of food, rents, and community services. Popular tourism areas tend to contribute to inflated prices for land or to environmental degradation, which can lead to further costs, as well as to the displacement of local populations. These added costs are sometimes referred to as *reverse multipliers*. The reverse multipliers associated with tourism are generally highest in areas that are isolated, have limited land available for expansion, or are dependent on importing food and other essentials from elsewhere. The most susceptible areas in this regard tend to be island and beach communities. Unfortunately, in many cases, these communities also tend to be among the areas most popular for high-density tourist development.

A truly rational approach to economic development would entail comparing tourism development with various other potential industries in terms of both their economic benefits and opportunity costs, selecting for investment those industries where the opportunity costs are low and the expected profits are high. An equitable approach, particularly important when public funds are to be invested, would also take into account the impact of reverse multipliers and call for comparisons as to how economic benefits can be expected to be distributed within a community. That economic criteria are seldom applied in such a fully rational manner is further testimony to the importance of other social and cultural forces in encouraging tourism development.

All industries are subject to patterns of *supply and demand*. The tourism industry is particularly vulnerable to shifts in demand. Travel patterns and tourist interests change over time, sometimes quickly and dramatically, as they might in response to changes in the political climate, health or security crises, or as a result of economic problems experienced by those countries that "supply" the most tourists. Small-scale and local tourism initiatives are often particularly vulnerable to shifts in demand. In some parts of the world, for example, threats or acts of violence toward tourists have resulted in a decline in tourist arrivals. While large chain hotels and similar facilities are usually able to weather such temporary setbacks, smaller locally owned operations may not have the resources to wait for more favorable conditions. In many places, tourism demand is also subject to considerable seasonal fluctuation. Popular recreational and beach areas sometimes operate at full capacity for only a few months out of a year. In these cases, employment in the tourist industry might not be a reliable form of employment for locals, who need year-round incomes. Tourism jobs are then taken up by transient workers, contributing less to the local economy. The summer employment of college students at beach resorts is a good example of this practice.

Most economists and tourism planners recognize that there are limits to the expansion of tourism facilities. Accordingly, they might try to measure a tourist location's *carrying capacity*, which is an expression of how many visitors might reasonably be accommodated in a given facility or region. The indices used to measure carrying capacity vary considerably and can be highly subjective and subject to cultural variation. Measuring capacity in relation to factors such as the number of hotel rooms available in a particular region is a fairly straightforward exercise, but trying to determine carrying capacity in respect to possible social or environmental impacts has proven to be much more difficult. What, for example, is the critical point at which the number of visitors to a region begins to result in a decline in the quality of life for the local population? There is no simple response to such a question. It depends on any number of factors, ranging from the practical, such as considerations of the capacity of a region's existing infrastructure, to more difficult to determine cultural differences in a community's capacity to tolerate strangers in its midst.

THE DISTRIBUTION OF ECONOMIC COSTS AND BENEFITS

Analyses of the economic benefits and costs of tourism has become a major tool for deciding where and how to encourage tourism development. However, as we have noted, such decisions are seldom based solely on economic criteria. They also include considerations of political power and prestige, as well as cultural attitudes related to a people's attitudes toward hospitality. One of the first comprehensive studies of the social impacts of tourism on developing countries is Emanuel De Kadt's (1979) *Tourism: Passport to Development?* This book is the result of research and collaboration sponsored by the World Bank during the 1970s. While the study notes that tourism has contributed substantially to the economic development of many Third World nations, the social consequences of tourism have varied widely. For example, in some cases, where tourism has contributed significantly to new employment and entrepreneurial opportunities, the result has included the creation of a new middle-income population of sufficient strength to challenge the political domination of a more traditional elite. In other instances, the new economic opportunities associated with tourism appear to have served the opposite effect, actually strengthening the economic and political hold of the elite. De Kadt's study describes other ways in which the economic benefits of tourism can have important implications for existing social structures. For example, in many places tourism has provided unprecedented employment opportunities for women and young people, with the potential to challenge the traditional male-dominated hierarchies of some of these places.

When considering the economics of tourism, anthropologists have often been most interested in the extent to which benefits are realized and costs are borne by the more marginal members of a population. They have noted that many promised benefits in terms of increased employment opportunities do not always occur. In some regions, for example, hotels and restaurants might decide to import experienced staff rather than bear the added cost of training local people. The economic costs associated with tourism can also be experienced disproportionately by marginal groups. Such costs might include increased prices for essential goods, displacement, and the loss of livelihood. Another important economic measure in this regard is related to how a region's *informal economic sector* operates. The informal economy is that part of a country's or region's economic development that is generally not supported by local authorities. Activities include hawking goods and tourist items on the street, providing unlicensed guide or transport services, participating in the black market, and various illegal activities such as petty theft and prostitution. These kinds of economic activities can be particularly important to marginal people. Countries and regions vary considerably in the extent to which they encourage or tolerate informal sector activities in relation to tourism. Interestingly enough, the more developed countries seem much less tolerant in this regard than do many of the less developed countries. In the United States, for example, strict control of business licensing, health and safety codes, and loitering laws have ensured that few informal sector activities develop in the vicinity of major tourist facilities. Many developing nations, on the other hand, have recognized the importance of the informal economy in providing badly needed employment opportunities. In these cases, authorities might actually support such activities, without officially sanctioning them.

The Sukimvit area is a well-known tourist haven in Bangkok, Thailand. The streets are lined with expensive shops and restaurants that much of the local population will never have the opportunity to visit. The sidewalks, on the other hand, are filled with vendors and hawkers offering any variety of tourist goods, from handicrafts to black-market cigarettes, to counterfeit brand-name products. Although the presence of so many vendors made it difficult for tourists to navigate the sidewalks, no effort was made to eliminate this part of the informal economy. Instead, the government decided to widen the sidewalks in order to create a "tourist walk." The unexpected result was a dramatic increase in vendors and hawkers, filling up the new sidewalks, and in many cases forcing the tourists to walk into the street to pass by. The only attempt the government made to curb this unanticipated tourist development was to declare one day a week as vendor free. This degree of toleration, based on a recognition of the important role played by the informal sector in Thailand's tourism economy, would be unheard of in most "developed" countries.

Another related factor that helps determine how economic benefits from tourism are distributed within a region has to do with the types of tourism that are offered. For years, the World Tourism Organization has advised developing nations that their best bet was to encourage "first-class" tourism in the form of major hotels and facilities that would attract wealthy visitors. The argument supporting this strategy is twofold. First, wealthy tourists obviously have more money to spend, and therefore a country or region needs to draw fewer visitors, reducing the possibly negative effects of having too many tourists hanging around. The potential social and cultural costs of tourism can, the argument goes, be further reduced by concentrating tourists in facilities reserved for their use, thereby minimizing contact between tourists and the local population. Although there may be some merit to this argument, there are other considerations that seem not to have been taken into account. As we have noted, first-class tourist facilities often rely heavily on foreign capital, and they generally require the provision of goods and services that are unlikely to be locally available, increasing the leakage of profits. Such facilities are also more likely to discourage if not prohibit the development of informal sector opportunities. Several tourism researchers have suggested that low-budget tourists have a more positive economic impact on the areas they visit than is often thought. They tend, for example, to rely much more on the local economy, seeking inexpensive meals and lodging that are more likely to have been provided by local entrepreneurs. One interesting study by economist Mark Hampton (1998) suggests that low-budget tourists may actually spend *more* in the long run than do first-class visitors, because, although they spend less on a daily basis, they usually stay in the countries they visit for a much longer time.

Although they pose problems in terms of the equitable distribution of tourism's benefits, the recommendations of the World Tourism Organization are backed by powerful incentives. The people who are most likely to benefit from first-class tourism development are those elites who are able to connect themselves with foreign capital and who, incidentally, are more likely to have the political clout to influence a region's tourism development planning. Questions of social class and ethnicity, expressed in terms of taste and style, play an important role in deciding what kinds of tourism to encourage. The facilities patronized by low-budget tourists might be viewed by a local elite as evidence of a region's "backwardness" and are therefore not likely to be supported. Low-budget tourists, often young and experimental in their behavior, might also represent lifestyle choices that local elite would prefer not to encourage. On the other hand, local elites are often eager to welcome "first-class" visitors and their facilities. In many developing areas, the grandest tourist hotels have also become centers where prominent local citizens gather to socialize and conduct their business.

To be fair, these kinds of discriminations are not always limited to local elites. Although there has been a fairly large amount of research devoted to trying to understand how local populations respond in general to tourism, there is little data available to help us differentiate these responses in relation to different segments of the local population or in respect to the kinds of tourism involved. I have noted the anecdote in which some Australian Aboriginal groups claimed to favor mass tourists over more culturally sensitive visitors, because the mass tourists were less intrusive. In a similar way, Gita Mehta's (1979) *Karma Cola* explores the local resentments occasioned in parts of India as a result of being inundated by youth from the West who are seeking their own uniquely spiritual experiences. More systematically designed research devoted to how local populations respond to different kinds of tourists is clearly needed.

Interest in tourism devoted to indigenous peoples has increased in recent years, partly as a result of the increased popularity of such kinds of tourism as ecotourism, adventure tourism, and heritage tourism. We will have an opportunity to consider the impact of tourism on indigenous people in the next two chapters. At this point, it is worth noting that two major tourism "commodities" have developed among indigenous groups. The first and most widespread of these is the marketing of indigenous culture, which often includes the selling of handicrafts, staged performances of "native" dances and ceremonies, and other opportunities to observe indigenous life. The second commodity has emerged in the United States, with the development of casino gambling on Native American lands. Since successfully resisting state government attempts to prohibit gambling on Native American reservations in the 1980s, high-stakes bingo and casino gaming has become the economic development preference of many Native American communities. The most successful gaming enterprise on tribal land has occurred on the Mashantucket Pequot reservation in Connecticut. In 1970, only two Pequot remained on the tribe's 200-acre reservation, and the state of Connecticut was on the verge of acquiring the land for a state park. Shortly thereafter, the Pequot reorganized their tribal government and, in 1983, they achieved federal recognition for their tribe. Numbering barely 300 members, the tribe began development of what was to become one of the largest casino operations in the world. By most accounts, the Pequot casino has proven to be an enormous benefit to the tribe, permitting them to expand their reservation and ensure the economic well-being of their members. Other Native American gaming initiatives have also contributed to economic development, although generally on a more modest basis, and not always as benignly as the Pequot experience. In some instances, for example, gaming has contributed to increased conflict among tribal members, as well as to increased crime on the reservations.

Although economic gain is rarely the only reason people encourage tourism development, it is still an important factor in such considerations. Tourism can be a lucrative business, and many regions of the world have used tourism to improve their economies and to compensate for declines in other revenue sources. In some instances, tourism has contributed positively to the economic well-being of minority and marginal populations. Other places have not fared so well, and the costs of tourism development have outweighed the hoped-for economic benefits. In other cases, there have been strikingly disproportionate distributions of the economic benefits associated with tourism. Unfortunately, competition for tourist dollars and added cultural and ideological "benefits" associated with tourism has sometimes led people to make unwise decisions.

TOURISM AS WORK

The economic incentives associated with tourism can be compelling in places where unemployment is high, as it is in many developing countries or in regions of more highly developed countries that are in decline, such as some rural areas and urban centers that have experienced an erosion of their industrial or agricultural base. Tourism provides employment opportunities in what is sometimes referred to as the *service sector* of the economy, which in many areas of the world has become the most rapidly growing sector for new employment.

The significance of added tourism employment varies from country to country and region to region. In a country like Singapore, for example, where employment and wages are high, low-end tourism employment opportunities (i.e., "minimum wage" jobs) provide little benefit to the local population and usually require the importation of labor from other countries. That is a troublesome prospect in this case, because Singapore's political leaders have attempted to maintain strong controls over the country's "ethnic balance." In other regions, where added employment opportunities are desperately needed, the typically low wages that are associated with most tourism employment can represent significant economic improvement over current conditions. The major obstacle to fully realizing these benefits in a local area is that potential employers might find that the local population lacks the skills necessary for employment. This is often the case when tourist development occurs in regions where the local population has had limited access to education and little previous experience in dealing with outsiders. While it is entirely possible to provide local residents with the kinds of training that would prepare them for tourism employment, employers often decide that it is easier to import already-skilled labor from other places.

Tourism employment is of interest to anthropologists for more than its relation to economic opportunity. Work is both shaped by and helps determine human social relations, and attitudes toward labor are invariably developed in cultural contexts. For example, anthropologists have noted that when tourism intrudes upon subsistence economies, it helps hasten a transition to wage-based labor, sometimes creating economic and social dependencies that did not exist before. New employment opportunities might also favor particular segments of a local population, resulting in alterations in a community's social structure. This can lead to changes in a community's power structure, in gender relations, and in relationships between ethnic groups. In Nepal, for example, trekking tourism opportunities have favored Sherpas, who are widely recognized for their reputations as guides. Other ethnic groups in the region have shared many of the costs associated with trekking tourism, but they have not realized proportionate benefits.

On the other hand, as Vicanne Adams (1992) notes, the Sherpas appear to have adapted well in their transition to increased dependence upon tourism wage labor. Before the arrival of large numbers of trekkers to the region, the Sherpas relied heavily upon principles of agricultural reciprocity, which served to define traditional modes of production and provide the basis for social interaction. Rather than abandoning these principles with increased dependency upon tourism, the Sherpas used their new-found wealth to reconstruct and in some instances actually strengthen their traditional patterns of economic and social relations.

There is considerable variation in the ways in which people of different regions adapt to tourism employment, and some of this variation undoubtedly relates to local and regional cultural patterns. Adjustment to tourism employment might be especially difficult where providing service to outsiders is likely to be associated with involuntary servitude, particularly if that servitude has in the past been imposed along the lines of racial or ethnic difference. In much of the Caribbean, for example, tourism has been characterized as a form of neocolonialism, serving to replicate many of the social and economic relationships of a racist past. Factors such as these can have important implications for the workers' attitudes toward tourism. They can also effect the way tourism is regarded by other locals who are not directly employed in the tourism industry.

Some observers have expressed concerns that tourism employment contributes to cultural homogenization when corporate and global patterns of work overtake local cultural differences in labor strategies and work ethics. There is other interesting evidence pointing to the ability of local work patterns to survive in adaptation to global expectations. In *Global Tourism and Informal Labour Relations*, Godfrey Baldacchino (1997) explores the effects of what he calls the "small-scale syndrome" on tourism work in the island nations of Barbados and Malta. Baldacchino studied labor relations at two major transnational tourist resorts on these islands. In such cases, we might anticipate that the work patterns of local workers employed by the resorts would easily be overwhelmed by the more global strategies of human resource management practiced by the resorts. But Baldacchino concludes that indigenous labor relations have played a major role in defining work roles and patterns in these new settings. A major feature of these informal practices is the role of personalistic social relations in establishing informal labor relations. While the corporations that manage the two resorts are oriented toward establishing objective, merit-based criteria for the promotion and recruitment of workers, the workers themselves have established informal criteria that rely more on considerations of kinship, social status, personal relations within the community, and allegiance to the community. In other words, it is still more important who you know and who you are within the indigenous social structure of these island microstates. Less important, according to Baldacchino, is how well you perform your job by any of the more objective, work-related standards established by the resorts. Baldacchino suggests that at least part of the reason that local patterns of social relationship prevail over corporate standards in these cases is because of the small-scale nature of island microstates. Even if they wanted to, workers would not be able to escape the prevailing social and political environments of their community, and it seems almost inevitable that these cultural identities should spill over into the workplace.

We can imagine a quite different scenario in other instances, in which individuals leave their communities to seek tourism employment elsewhere. In these cases, workers have lost the support of their personal networks and escaped the ascriptive criteria for social relations that serve to maintain their home communities. Tourism workers in these situations are surely more vulnerable to standards of labor relations that are imposed by the tourism facilities. This provides, of course, another reason that the managers of tourism facilities might prefer outside labor over employing locals.

TOURISM POLICIES AND PLANS

Tourism is realized through a variety of political processes. Most governments establish tourism policies that reflect both their cultural and economic ambitions as well as their concerns over the potential impacts of tourism. These policies are formulated internationally, at the level of the nation-state, and on down through the political activities of local communities. Attempts to transform policies into realities are further expressed through varieties of planning processes, in which governments and other actors attempt to determine the kinds of tourism to be encouraged, the places where tourists will be welcomed, and the ways in which both tourism development and tourist behaviors are regulated. Most tourism policies and plans result from coalitions between government and the private sector, and the amount of influence wielded by one or the other of these actors varies considerably from place to place. Tourism development is also subject to numerous other kinds of governmental concern, such as trade and monetary policy, environmental and land use regulations, and laws governing human behavior.

Not all of the politics associated with tourism originates with governmental authorities or results solely from the interactions of public-sector facilitators and private-sector business interests. Some of the most dramatic and spontaneous instances of political behavior arise from local, grassroots responses to tourism, in which community members are often pitted against each other in support of or in opposition to tourism initiatives. Neither is tourism simply a passive product of governmental interests. It has the capability of influencing political processes and altering governments. The wealth generated by successful tourism ventures can, for example, bring new actors into the political arena, resulting in shifts in power from a traditional elite to a new entrepreneurial class. In other cases, however, traditional elites have managed to strengthen their position by stifling competition and maintaining control of the new wealth generated by tourism. Some measure of how important a role tourism has come to play in the politics of many regions is provided by the extent to which tourists have become the target of terrorist activities. In places as diverse as the Philippines, Uganda, Egypt, and Aspen, Colorado, marginalized political groups and radical special interests have chosen to mount their political protests in the form of attacks on tourists and tourist facilities.

Although we might argue as to the true purposes of modern, bureaucratic governments, certainly one of their major functions is to make plans. We live in a political and social environment that seems unable to exist without a future. An industry as large and complex as tourism gives rise to complex planning and development strategies. Inadequate planning can lead to such problems as poor market response (not enough tourists to justify expenditures), strains on the infrastructure and environment of popular tourist destinations, inadequate personnel to service a growing tourist industry, unacceptable leakage of profits, and local community resentment toward tourists. Planning is often necessary at later as well as early stages of tourism development. Postdevelopment planning activities might include monitoring the impacts of tourism, redirecting tourism initiatives to attract different kinds of tourists, "capping" tourist densities in particular areas, and reconsiderations of the ways in which the profits from tourism are distributed within a society.

Tourism planning occurs at many different levels. International planning related to tourism is conducted by transnational corporations and through the negotiations of cooperating trading block countries, as well as by various professional and human service organizations such as the World Tourism Organization, the United Nations, and the World Bank. Planning also occurs with varying degrees of intensity at national, provincial, and community levels. Private-sector interests related to the tourism industry—such as travel agencies, hotels, and airlines—also engage in planning at several levels and in association with the government agencies that regulate their activities. In attempting to understand the significance of tourism planning to any particular region of the world, it is important to understand the kinds of relationships that have developed between these different levels and sectors of influence. It is also important to recognize that countries and regions differ in terms of which levels and sectors tend to dominate tourism planning.

In some countries where government is highly centralized, tourism planning is frequently dominated by the national government. This is often the case in developing nations. A major advantage of such a centralized approach is its efficiency. National governments exercise considerable discretion as to how they promote and market tourism as well as to how they direct tourism development to different regions of the country. This is a particular advantage in the early stages of tourism development, where promoting and marketing a country's tourism resources is critical. On the other hand, a major disadvantage of highly centralized planning is that cooperation with local and regional authorities might be more difficult to initiate or maintain. As social, environmental, and infrastructural problems begin to occur on the local level, they are more difficult to correct.

In other countries, such as the United States, the most active tourism planning occurs at the level of state and local governments. A major advantage of this more decentralized approach is that most tourism planning occurs close to the locations where tourism takes place. For this reason, it is usually easier to maintain public support for tourism and to anticipate local environmental and infrastructural problems that are likely to arise as a result of tourism development. A disadvantage of this approach is that it can be less efficient, especially in terms of marketing and promotion, involving considerably more competition between regions.

It is also useful to look at the relationships between public and private sectors for tourism planning. In the United States, the private domain is an active participant in formal tourism planning. Local Chambers of Commerce and other business associations play an important role. In many United States cities, local business associations take the lead in tourism promotion, with city governments following their lead. In some other countries, the government dominates tourism planning. Here, business interests tend to play a more informal role in planning, often as a result of personalistic links to government elites.

Not all tourism development occurs as a result of deliberate planning. Planned development *anticipates* changes related to tourism development, while unplanned development *responds* to changes in tourism opportunities. An interesting case in point is the way in which tourism has developed on the Indonesian island of Bali. During the 1960s, the Indonesian government targeted Bali for major international tourism development. The government's plan was to limit development to a small part of the island and to concentrate on providing beachside accommodations for first-class tourists. The effort was successful enough to generate considerable international interest in Bali as a desirable travel location. When tourists who desired something other than a "first-class" experience began to show up, the Balinese themselves were quick to respond by providing additional, low-cost accommodations (*losmen*) for more bud-get-minded travelers. These accommodations were generally family operated and locally owned, and they rapidly became available through-out the island. This resulted in an expansion of tourism throughout Bali as well as significantly increased local employment opportunities. In this case, unplanned tourism development might be judged in a positive light, in that it has served to redistribute a considerable portion of the profit from tourism to local entrepreneurs. In other cases, the results of unplanned tourist development, such as environmental degradation, overcrowding, and increased crime, might be judged in a more negative way.

The policies and plans that are associated with tourism develop-ment almost invariably represent more than economic considerations. It can be argued that wealth, particularly when its acquisition rises above subsistence needs, is seldom an end in and of itself. Rather, wealth pro-vides a means of achieving culturally significant goals that are expressed through human values and lifestyle choices. Thus, for example, economic development might be seen as a means of maintaining the cultural integ-rity of a group, of achieving social and cultural dominance over other groups, and of expressing individual and group identity. In some instances, and this seems apparent in many tourism activities, the aims of economic development might actually be subordinate to other cultural and political ambitions. This is one of the more tacit dimensions of tour-ism. As we will see later in this chapter, promises of economic develop-ment can sometimes serve as a ruse for other political and cultural ben-efits that are not likely to enter into public discourse because of their con-troversial and hegemonic intentions.

TRANSNATIONAL DIMENSIONS OF TOURISM

It is no secret that the international tourism industry is dominated by "sender" countries. Senders are the relatively wealthy places that pro-vide the greater number of international tourists and also supply much of the capital and material for tourism development. While many aspects of this domination are controlled by private-sector corporations that rep-resent the travel and hospitality industries, they also require govern-ment-to-government negotiations. Sender governments, for example, ne-gotiate with host governments for favorable trade agreements concern-ing airline competition and the provision of tourism goods and services. On the other hand, many host governments attempt to place restrictions on the flow of international capital, as well as on the ownership of tour-ism facilities. These kinds of political negotiations occur at high levels of government and often involve considerations that extend well beyond those of tourism development. Concessions in granting aircraft landing rights or in allowing a major transnational hotel chain to enter a region are, for example, often linked to other nontouristic trade-offs related to trade negotiations between countries. In this sense, transnational tourism-related negotiations seldom follow a course that is based solely on considerations of the specific merits or disadvantages of tourism development. They also require attention to the overall status of trade negotiations and political relations between countries.

Transnational tourism negotiations are not limited to considerations of economic advantage and balance of trade. Airlines and other tourist facilities, such as Hilton hotels and Disney theme parks, also represent powerful national symbols. When a country's airlines and hospitality industries cross national borders, their reception in host countries becomes a matter of national concern in ways that are seldom realized in a domestic context. In a sense, the "ownership" of these industries is transferred from the private to the public sector. The refusal of a host country to allow in-country flights of a foreign airline can become, for example, more than an issue of trade negotiation. It can as easily be interpreted as an act of subtle aggression toward the country that the airline represents. In a more extreme example, terrorist acts against airlines and international hotels are seldom viewed as attacks against the corporations that own them, but rather as assaults upon the nations they represent. This, of course, is often the clear intent of the terrorist group.

A country's citizens also can be seen as representative of a national presence. Many governments have a long history of looking after the safety of their citizens when they travel beyond their borders. For example, early colonial-era trade negotiations between Western nations and other countries made strict provisions for the safety of travelers, including in some cases restricting the rights of host countries to prosecute Westerners for violations of local laws. While such international agreements are no longer in force, except in the limited case of diplomatic immunity, their customs are sometimes still practiced informally. Host countries that have experienced periods of political domination by Western powers, and which still experience economic domination, are often more likely to expel rather than prosecute Western tourists who violate their laws.

Those countries that supply large numbers of tourists can have important impacts on other countries' tourism potential, particularly in the extent to which they encourage or discourage their citizens to visit particular regions. In some instances, travel is prohibited altogether or made so difficult as to make it impractical for the casual tourist—this has been the case, for example, of travel between the United States and Cuba. Travel can be discouraged with the use of travelers' advisories that alert citizens to health and safety problems in other countries. The

United States Department of State routinely lists countries in which they feel their citizens might become the victims of crime or civil strife. Just as regularly, the listed countries protest that the State Department's assessments are less than objective and often based on ideological and political considerations. For their part, host countries often apply political and cultural considerations to the ways they regulate tourist arrivals. They might do this by carefully selecting those countries in which they promote themselves as a tourist destination, by granting differential landing rights for different countries' airlines, and by easing or tightening visa restrictions for citizens of different countries.

The transnational politics of tourism are not limited to relations between historically dominant countries and less powerful countries. Provisions regarding tourism development figure prominently in negotiations between countries of equal or near equal power. There has been a growing tendency for countries to enter into regional cooperative alliances in order to increase their competitive advantage in the global marketplace. A major goal of these pacts has been to cooperate in trade and economic ventures, including tourism development. In some regions, these cooperative activities have the potential to alter tourism development in significant ways—by easing travel restrictions between member nations, by encouraging capital exchange, and even by initiating new tourism opportunities that translate these new economic alliances into cultural expressions. An example of the latter is the emphasis on generic *European*—as opposed to national—tourism development since the establishment of the European Union. New tourism initiatives supported by the European Council clearly support the political goal of unification. For example, one such development has been the inauguration of a series of cultural routes that cut across national borders and emphasize continuities in the European experience. A tourist can travel throughout Europe visiting public gardens, tracing the development of the textile industry as a distinctly European enterprise, following historical pilgrimage routes, or indulging one of several other themes. This is an excellent example of the ways in which the political aims of a tourism enterprise might have considerable influence on ways in which tourism is developed. The goal of the European Council's cultural tourism routes is to encourage Europeans, and presumably other visitors, to envision their heritage in European terms rather than strictly as a result of national or local experience. If this type of tourism experience were to become popular and widely practiced, it would also encourage a shift in the way Europeans and visitors travel through Europe, with less emphasis upon what is sometimes referred to as "destination" tourism and greater attention to "corridor" tourism, in which the trip itself, rather than what awaits at the end of the line, becomes the major goal of a touristic experience.

Tourism can encourage cooperation between nations, as well as promote understanding among people of different lands. Such diverse transnational organizations as the United Nations, the World Bank, and the World Travel Organization have on various occasions alluded to tourism as a mechanism for world peace. Tourism has been lauded for its capacity to encourage greater understanding among peoples as a result of the exchange of visitors. It can also encourage countries to cooperate in order to realize the benefits of tourism and provide an incentive to avoid violent conflict that would reduce the number of visitors to an area. The extent to which these assumptions can be proven true is bound to vary from one type of tourism experience to another. Some tourism scholars have noted, for example, that international travel does not always lead to greater understanding among peoples, particularly in those frequent instances in which there are considerable economic or cultural differences between host and guest countries. In some cases, tourism might just as easily contribute to a strengthening of cultural stereotypes and to increased misunderstandings.

In *The Politics of Tourism in Asia*, Linda Richter (1989) has noted that tourism policy is nearly always a part of modern trade and cooperative agreements between nations. Where countries have been in conflict, agreements regarding tourism are often the first initiatives to indicate "normalization" between these countries. For example, tourism-related considerations have figured prominently in recent security talks between Israel and the Palestinian Liberation Organization. In this case, guarantees of access to religious and historically significant sites were a major concern of the negotiations.

Geopolitical boundaries sometimes serve in their own right as tourist attractions. Political frontiers might, for example, attract visitors in pursuit of inexpensive or tariff-free goods or draw others who wish to engage in activities that are prohibited in their home territories but allowed just across a border. Political boundaries have also given rise to distinct cultural entities that attract tourists. In the United States, for example, parts of the "Tex-Mex" border provide a unique ambiance—complete with its own cuisine, attractions, and historical markers—that is enjoyed by many visitors. Another such border region is Southeast Asia's "Golden Triangle," encompassing the borders of Burma, Thailand, and Laos. Here, adventuresome visitors are provided with the opportunity to trek among ethnic villagers, perhaps "sneak" across national borders, and, if they wish, to partake of the region's most infamous product, opium. Borders, like the travel depots and terminals I eluded to at the beginning of this book, are interesting places to many people because they are so thoroughly representative of transience and of the mixture of distinct cultural elements.

The transnational aspects of tourism can have a bearing on the development of individual nation-states. We have already considered how some aspects of modern tourism can be traced to travel concessions that colonial powers wrested from the governments over which they had established dominance. These same concessions have also sometimes served to strengthen the governments that did yield to colonial influence. For example, when the Western powers entered Southeast Asia, it became common practice for Western travelers to secure documents from regional political leaders that assured their safety while journeying throughout the country. In reality, these local political leaders often had much less authority over the regions that were supposedly under their control than seemed apparent to the Western powers. By agreeing to guarantee travel rights into territories that were quasi-independent, the local leaders were afforded the opportunity to test their sovereignty in ways that had not yet been recognized. Nineteenth-century Western travelers to the hinterlands of Thailand (then Siam) reported that the local lords and tribal chiefs they encountered were often puzzled by the letters of safe passage that had been provided by the king of Siam, and openly questioned whether the king had the authority to extend his guarantees into their realms.

Tourism continues to play a role in establishing the authority of the rulers of many developing nations. Typically, international travelers arrive in a country as guests of the nation, with the same apparent guarantees of safety and convenience that were once assured a much smaller group of travelers by letters of safe passage. As these tourists move about in a country, they unwittingly serve as representatives of the nation-state. In particularly remote regions, tourism might well be one of the most apparent indicators of state control, justifying the need to build roads and facilities and providing incentives for further state intervention into local bases of authority. In some countries, for example, separate state-controlled police forces have been established both to protect tourists and to regulate their behavior. These "tourist police" serve in many instances to extend state control over local jurisdictions, as well as to provide tourists with some of the special privileges and statuses that were earlier recognized in agreements with colonial governments.

THE POLITICS OF REPRESENTATION

Nationalism remains a pervasive force in the modern world, and its association with tourism can be represented in several ways. The business of making a nation is to convince or compel citizens to accept the idea that the interests of the nation should prevail over other cultural, social, and regional interests. This struggle to capture competing allegiances can be expressed in quite crude ways, as through the use of force, but it is also and routinely conveyed by more subtle means, through the use and manipulation of symbols.

In *Recovered Roots,*Yael Zerubavel (1995) describes the transition of the Israeli shrine at Masada from a sacred site that represented a unique moment in Jewish history to a more secularized place that celebrates Israeli nationalism. Masada is the site of a Jewish fortress that was conquered by Romans in A.D. 73. Zerubavel argues that with the encouragement of tourism to Masada the original, internal symbolism of the shrine has been diminished. Tourism permits outsiders to partake in a passive manner in ceremonies that once required the active participation of everyone present. The transition of Masada from a mostly local pilgrimage place to a tourist site was accomplished in part with the construction of cable cars. Before this, the shrine was accessible only by an arduous climb to the summit. For many Israelis, the climb represented the struggle of Masada's original inhabitants. Much of the special meaning of this pilgrimage has been eroded by the presence of numerous tourists who arrive at the site by cable car.

Zerubavel suggests that tourism at Masada is a triumph of secular national interests over more localized and religious interests. It is equally possible to find places in which tourism has been used to contest the interpretation of national symbols. The Alamo is a popular shrine that has served to symbolize the independence of Texas from Mexico and further represents the incorporation of Texan identity into an anglicized United States nationhood. Custody of the Alamo and control over its symbolic representation as a tourist site is maintained by the Daughters of the Republic of Texas. In her book *Inherit the Alamo*, Holly Beachley Brear (1995) has chronicled an alternative interpretation of the site by citizens who feel that the region's Hispanic heritage is being misrepresented in the shrine's focus upon a story in which "good Anglos" managed to prevail over "evil Hispanics." Hispanic groups have not only called for a broader and more inclusive interpretation of the site itself, but have staged alternative tourist-oriented ceremonies and demonstrations off the site of the Alamo.

In some cases, the stakes involved in representing nationalistic claims through tourism can be quite high. For example, recent tourism in Taiwan has included the promotion of ethnic tourism focused on the cultural minorities that occupied the island (then Formosa) before the Nationalist Chinese entered in 1949. The attempt to associate these minority groups with Taiwanese national identity serves in a powerful way to extend Taiwan's claim for independence from mainland China. Interestingly enough, in developing ethnic heritage sites in the south of China, mainland Chinese government officials also chose to emphasize ethnic groups that were closely related to indigenous Formosan peoples, implying thereby an even lengthier historical association with the mainland (Oakes 1998).

As we saw in the case of the Alamo, the politics of representation are often expressed on the local level as different parts of a community become engaged in efforts to promote, resist, or gain control of touristic activities. The development of Baltimore's Inner Harbor as a major tourist attraction provides a case in point. Baltimore's Inner Harbor Marketplace has become a much emulated model for urban redevelopment. To appreciate its political significance, we need to understand the conditions under which the project was conceived and the way its development proceeded.

During the 1960s, Baltimore was a city on the decline. Like many other "rust belt" cities, it had steadily lost much of its industrial base to the rapidly growing "sun belt" cities, many of which offered generous tax breaks and other incentives to industries that were willing to relocate. At the same time, the city was experiencing a change in the makeup of its population. The number of black citizens was increasing at the same time as increasing numbers of whites were leaving the city. By the late 1960s, Baltimore's majority population had become black. At the same time, employment possibilities for the city's populace continued to decline, and political control of the city continued to be in the hands of a white minority. In 1968, with the assassination of the Reverend Martin Luther King, Jr., the frustrations of Baltimore's black population, like those in many U.S. cities, erupted into a series of demonstrations and riots.

At this low point, local politicians took a two-prong approach to solving the city's problems. To attempt to counter the disturbing racial divide, city leaders decided to hold a city fair that would emphasize Baltimore's "unity through diversity." Every community in the city was invited to participate in the fair by contributing a booth in which community members were to describe the positive features of their neighborhoods. It was decided that the city fair would be held at Baltimore's Inner Harbor, which at the time was a mostly abandoned port area several blocks from the city's commercial center. The second initiative was to redevelop the declining city center, which gravitated around Charles Street, one of the major south-to-north routes through the city.

At first, these two initiatives were seen as independent of each other. The city fair would hopefully help heal some of the internal rifts that had divided the city's citizens. It was seen primarily as a *local* celebration. On the other hand, the development of what came to be known as the downtown Charles Center was seen mostly as a project of the business community and as an effort to attract outside investors. Because the business community was composed of both city businesses and other financial interests that were located in the surrounding Baltimore County, this initiative was seen largely as a *regional* activity.

What happened next is a good example of how difficult it can be to anticipate the course of any kind of development. First of all, the city fair was far more successful than its planners had envisioned. Not only did it draw a large number of local citizens, but from the start it also attracted many tourists, who came to witness this unique display of the city's diverse neighborhood traditions. By its second year, more than a million persons attended the fair—more than the city's entire population. The surprising success of the city fair in attracting outsiders drew the attention of potential investors. One such person, a developer named Charles Rouse, proposed that the city redirect some its development initiatives to the Inner Harbor. He offered to create a "festival marketplace" that would include shopping and entertainment facilities in a celebratory atmosphere—a permanent and much more commercialized and tourist-oriented version of the popular city fair.

The next twenty years of the Inner Harbor's development and its success as a landmark of "urban renaissance" is a complex matter that requires more detail than can be provided here. For our purposes, the most important aspect of the Inner Harbor's transformation into a major tourist destination is the ensuing conflict between the site as a place for local celebration and as a place for regional and tourist celebration. As the Inner Harbor became a popular tourist destination, local decision makers began to view its original, local significance as being in conflict with the new festival atmosphere. Events such as the city fair clearly emphasized the city's increasing "blackness." Developers of the Inner Harbor now sought an image that was more reflective of the kind of tourist experience they wanted to encourage, which would in many respects provide an escape from, rather than a confrontation with, urban realities. The idea of the festival marketplace was to provide entertainment and shopping in an atmosphere that visitors would feel was fun-filled, relaxed, and safe. Developers came to regard the city fair, which had begun to attract large numbers of inner-city black youth to the Inner Harbor, as being incompatible with the idea of festival they had in mind. As a result, the city fair was relocated to a space on the periphery of the new Inner Harbor developments. Shortly after that, it was moved even further from the Harbor, to a space underneath a highway overpass. Finally, the city fair was moved all the way across town, far from the city's now-thriving tourism center, to the parking lot of an abandoned school. It lasted there for only two more years, after which its sponsors declared the city fair to be defunct.

Communities frequently experience conflicts related to tourism. In many cases these conflicts are related to much more deeply rooted differences. For example, tourism has not created racial divisions in Baltimore but has developed within the context of racial discrimination and to some extent serves to reinforce race-based conflicts. One very effective way that tourism serves this purpose is that it "justifies" discrimination as a necessity of doing business. Baltimore's increasing "blackness" has to be muted because it does not have touristic appeal. Many outsiders might actually be frightened away should Baltimore's Inner Harbor appear to be too black. While no public official or tourism developer would be likely to admit to this kind of reasoning, the pattern of the Inner Harbor development leaves little doubt as to its influence. The racial politics of Baltimore are such that tourism helps to maintain the balance of political authority in favor of continued control by a traditional white elite, precisely at the point that internal city politics had begun to tip in favor of a new black majority. Tourism is a relatively safe kind of racial politics because it is shaped in great part by assumptions of what outsiders desire. Presumably, the city's new image is no longer an expression of the dominance of one segment of the community, but is rather an image formed in respect to the "tourist gaze." To give tourists what they want is just good business practice, from which (presumably, again) everyone will benefit. Thus, tourism planners are relieved of responsibility for the kinds of images and types of facilities they have supported.

Tourism can play an important role in both national and local politics because it tends to reinforce existing patterns of dominance and political control, while at the same time deflecting that dominance as an expression of what tourists require. It is interesting to note that local resentment toward tourists is generally high in locations in which elite political dominance is most apparent. While there might be good reason to resent some of the actions of tourists, in many cases a part of this resentment is actually an expression of a greater dissatisfaction with the exercise of power on the part of those national and local elites who have fostered tourism development. In some intense political situations, where direct confrontations with the political elite are discouraged and often severely dealt with, it can be much safer to direct one's dissatisfaction toward people like tourists, who are presumably outside the political domain.

The development of Baltimore's Inner Harbor provides an example of the way in which the politics of representation can serve the interests of a political elite. Touristic representations can also be employed to resist these same hegemonic processes. Local, grassroots tourism initiatives are sometimes developed in direct opposition to particularly potent symbols of local power. This was the case, for example, when San Antonio's Hispanic community began to provide alternative ceremonies that represented their interpretations of the significance of the Alamo.

Grassroots tourism developments might also occur in the absence of such singular tourist icons. Sharon Macdonald (1997) has provided such a case in her study of the development of a local heritage center on the Isle of Skye, in the Scottish Hebrides. Skye has long been a popular European tourist destination. The Aros heritage center was developed by local entrepreneurs to provide visitors with a better understanding of the region's distinct Gaelic heritage as well as to instill a sense of local pride in that heritage. The center's two principal developers had been active in larger political efforts to encourage the speaking of Gaelic in Scotland. Although Macdonald admits that the heritage center represents an instance of the commodification of culture for tourist consumption, she maintains that its supporters have been able to draw a clear distinction between commodity exchange, which involves giving up ownership of something, and a sense of "inalienable possessions" (e.g., Weiner 1992), in which objects and images that are exchanged continue to retain their intrinsic identities with their place of origin. In other words, Macdonald asserts that the people of Skye have been able to "sell" their culture to tourists while at the same time increasing its local value.

Much of the politics of tourism is invested in attempts to draw the visitor's attention to particular interpretations of a place or region. To the extent that such attempts are successful, the outsider's acceptance of an interpretation serves to help confirm its "authenticity" and to strengthen the interpreters' claims to represent local symbols and their histories. As we noted earlier in this chapter, the cultural and ideological benefits associated with this process can in many instances outweigh the presumed economic benefits of particular tourism developments.

SOCIAL CONSEQUENCES OF TOURISM

We have already explored several ways in which tourism might contribute to social change. Opportunities for tourism employment can, for example, lead to alterations in the structure of authority in a community. Tourists can introduce new or intensified social practices to a region, ranging from different standards of hospitality to prostitution and illegal drug use. In some cases, tourism might also reinforce existing social relations, particularly where traditional social activities such as festivals and performances become tourist attractions—although, in such instances, the local meanings assigned to these events might well be altered as a result of the participation of outsiders. Where tourism constitutes a major new source of revenue within a community or region, it might contribute to increased social distance and inequality between those members of the community who directly benefit from tourism and others who do not.

Tourism can also have an effect on the ethnic balance of a community. In the case of Baltimore's Inner Harbor, we noted how the city's African-American presence has been marginalized in part as a result of decisions concerning tourism development. In this case, tourists' preferences were *assumed* to be in conformity with prevailing local attitudes toward race. In other instances, tourists' actual preferences might have considerable impact. This was true, for example, of tourism pertaining to trekking in Nepal, in which tourist preferences for Sherpa guides served to alter relations between the Sherpa and other local ethnic groups. In other instances, the impacts of tourism on local ethnic structures can be considerably less direct. For example, Isaac Sindiga (1996) has described a case in which one Kenyan ethnic group has become increasingly marginalized within its regional economy as a result of its reluctance to participate in international tourism. Sindiga points out that the Waswahili have in the past played an important role in the development of Kenya's coastal economy. They have, however, avoided participating in tourism development on the grounds that tourist behaviors (such as alcohol consumption and sexual promiscuity) conflict with their Muslim beliefs. As tourism becomes an increasingly important segment of Kenya's overall economic development, the Waswahili's overall participation in the economy has declined. Sindiga suggests that this increased marginalization has contributed to a resurgence of Islamic fundamentalism among the Waswahili, adding to local ethnic conflict.

Compared to the amount of scholarship that has been devoted to trying to discern different motivations and types of tourists, relatively little comparative research has been directed to attempting to generalize the ways in which communities and regions respond to tourism. One exception is Hasan Zafer Dogan's (1989) article on "Forms of Adjustment," in which he describes several ideal types of strategies that communities employ in response to the presence of tourists. Dogan suggests, for example, that some communities actively *resist* tourism and attempt to discourage tourist visits. This might be the predominant response in regions where there is a long history of conflict between residents and outsiders, as would be true of many colonial situations, or where the social practices of tourists are likely to violate local norms. Other communities might be more likely to *retreat* from tourism by tolerating the presence of tourists but trying to avoid contact as much as possible. Dogan indicates that this type of response can occur in a region where community members recognize the economic importance of tourism but seek to avoid the social consequences of having strangers in their midst. "Retreating" from tourism might take the form of a general opposition to modernization or result in attempts to maintain or revive local traditions.

A third type of response to tourism is *boundary maintenance*, in which a community actively encourages tourism but also tries to maintain a strict line between activities related to tourism and those related to the maintenance of local social structure. Boundaries might be maintained by creating special places for tourists and discouraging them from entering private spaces or by making strict distinctions between those aspects of a culture that are produced specifically for tourists and those that are reserved for local consumption. Dogan notes, for example, that many Balinese communities deliberately alter the "traditional" dances they perform for tourists, as a way of preserving the religious significance of the dances they perform amongst themselves. Another kind of response is evident when communities use tourism to *revitalize* local customs and traditions. Dogan notes ways in which tourism has encouraged communities to revive traditional handicrafts, arts and ceremonies, as well as contributed to increased interest in the preservation of historic structures and places.

Finally, a fifth possible response to tourism is *adoption*, in which community members freely substitute parts of their traditional culture with new attitudes and customs introduced by tourists. Dogan suggests that adoption is especially likely to be the strategy preferred by younger members of a society. We might note, however, that adoption is also not uncommon among social elites, where tourism and its facilities are often embraced as symbols of development and modernization.

Dogan cautions that his five types of adjustment to tourism are ideal and that in reality most communities practice a variety of the types. He also notes that the adjustments are unevenly distributed within most communities, depending in part on social and cultural differences and on differences in the extent to which particular segments of a population perceive themselves as directly benefiting from tourism.

In his edited volume, *Coping with Tourists: European Reactions to Mass Tourism*, Jeremy Boissevan (1996) argues that the negative social impacts of tourism are often overstated, particularly in regard to tourism in the developed countries of Europe. He suggests that many accounts of tourism leave the erroneous impression that local communities and regions are without adequate social or political resources to effectively "cope" with the changes brought by tourism. Boissevan is especially interested in how local residents defend the "back regions" or private spheres of their communities from tourist incursion. He describes six coping strategies.

The first strategy is *covert resistance*. Boissevan notes that relations between tourists and those who provide tourist services are often unequal. Tourists tend to be wealthy and influential, and most tourism workers are not. Forms of covert resistance include gossiping about and stereotyping tourists in less than favorable ways, obstructing and deliberately misleading tourists, and displays of rudeness toward tourists. Boissevan maintains that such behaviors help people who are placed in a subordinate position maintain their self-respect.

Another strategy for coping with tourists is *hiding*. This might involve scheduling important community festivities and events at times when tourists are unlikely to be present, during "off season" or at times of the day when tourists are otherwise occupied. Some aspects of a culture might be deliberately withheld from tourist consumption. Boissevan cites particular kinds of local food as an example. He also notes that, where important local events and ceremonies have drawn the attention of tourists, there is often a tendency among community members to create new "insider-only" celebrations, from which tourists are excluded. Guides and local guidebooks can also assist a community in hiding aspects of its culture by excluding certain places from their recommended tours. In this respect, it is worth considering the perhaps unintended impacts of some alternative guidebooks, such as the popular

Lonely Planet series, which are devoted in great part to directing tourists to a place's back regions.

Boissevan's third coping strategy is *fencing*. This can involve creating material barriers in order to ensure privacy or moving an activity that has attracted the interest of tourists to some other place. In some cases, tourists might be physically barred from entering particular areas. Fencing strategies serve to inform tourists of the limits of their participation. Another strategy for coping with tourism is *ritual*. Ritual performances are ways to celebrate community identity and deal with uncertainty. Boissevan argues that the creation and performance of local rituals has increased dramatically throughout Europe and suggests that this is in part a reaction to the uncertainties and threats to local identity that are introduced by tourism.

The two final coping strategies described by Boissevan are those of *organized protest* and *aggression*. Protests might be directed toward tourists. For an example, Boissevan cites an instance in which a priest in a Maltese village organized parishioners to protest against tourists whose revealing apparel were offensive to local customs. Organized protests might also be directed toward those who mediate tourism, such as hoteliers who intrude upon public places or agencies that organize sex tours. Aggression takes the form of violence against tourists. What Boissevan is describing here is not the kind of violence that might occur in the commission of other tourist-related crimes, such as robbery, but rather aggressive acts that result directly from community members' resentment toward the behavior or attitudes of tourists. He cites an example in which a European tourist was stoned to death for photographing a carnival performance in Chiapas, Mexico.

The mechanisms described by Dogan and Boissevan point to social changes that result from community responses to tourism. In these cases, the differences between being a tourist and being a "host" seem quite clear. In many other instances, however, the distinction can be much more ambiguous. The categories of tourist and host are socially constructed and, while much of the literature (including many of parts of this book) treat them as fairly distinct categories, they are in reality quite mutable. The scholarly literature has tended to focus on events of tourism as they relate to particular places or to pay attention to the act of being a tourist, rather than investigate the processes through which touring and hosting are defined. In general, the study of tourism has favored instances in which the categories of tourist and host are differentiated in part on the basis of such factors as wealth, nationality, and social or cultural distance. There are more studies of international tourism than there are of domestic tourism, for example, and many tourism researchers seem to assume that touring is a privilege enjoyed by only a portion of the world's people. Anthropologists tend to focus on touristic situations that involve even greater differences between tourists and the communities they visit. In other words, the kinds of tourism we normally choose to study are those in which the distinctions between host and guest seem quite clear and unproblematic.

As a whole, however, tourism is much more of a reciprocal endeavor than we might first imagine. It is one in which people frequently exchange the roles of tourist and toured. This is, for example, a common feature of domestic tourism. In her discussion of Japanese domestic tourism to the village of Kuzaki, famous for its women pearl divers, D. P. Martinez (1990) notes that the villagers' accommodation of tourists is related in part to the fact that the villagers do not see themselves as all that different from their visitors. Their relationships with the people who visit their village are shaped in part by their own identities as tourists to other places:

> When the people of Kuzaki go on holiday, they love to go drinking and dancing in the big cities like Kyoto or Tokyo. They are also interested in the search for unusual and exotic places in Japan; especially the men, who believe that women in other places might be more interesting than their own. The women of Kuzaki, as well, like to see what the shrines, temples and 'geisha' in other places are like. [The villagers] on holiday have many of the same expectations as do the tourists who come to their villages. They are as capable of practising 'touristic imperialism' as are the visitors to their village which says a great deal about the universality of the touristic experience . . . they too are caught up in this search for the real and authentic Japan; a Japan which they both represent and continue to look for in other places. (p. 111)

It can sometimes be difficult to distinguish tourists from the local population. This is especially true, for example, in urban areas, where tourists and residents are often involved in the same activities, eating at the same restaurants, and visiting the same sites and attractions. At Baltimore's Inner Harbor, discussed earlier, local businesspeople and tourists rub shoulders at lunchtime, and residents and visitors frequent the same nightclubs and speciality stores. While residents might on occasion resent the influx of visitors to these places, and the traffic problems and overcrowding that results, they also benefit from being able to share in a greater variety of attractions, public places, and eateries than could be supported solely by their patronage. In cases such as the Inner Harbor, of course, many of these benefits are unequally realized, because such places tend to be expensive and beyond the means of many other local residents.

There are other kinds of tourism experiences in which the category of "host" becomes problematic. In the United States, for example, a large proportion of the tourism workers at beach resort towns are not from the local area at all. College students, among others, often seek summer employment at such places, and in doing so they come to occupy a special category that fits somewhere between tourist and host. Another quite different example is provided by Margaret Kenna (1993) in her study of tourism on a small Greek island. Kenna points out that most of the tourism development on the island is controlled by first- and second-generation return migrants. While a tourist is likely to regard these migrants as locals, long-term residents of the island are more likely to think of them as outsiders. The return migrants' control of the tourism industry on the island has served to limit the participation of long-term residents and contributed to increased social and economic stratification on the island.

There are numerous other social consequences of tourism development. Tourism can contribute to increases in criminal activity in a local community (e.g., Pizam and Mansfeld 1996). In some cases, crime is directed toward tourists, who are especially vulnerable as a result of their unfamiliarity with local places and practices. Tourists might also be preferred prey for property crimes because local criminals realize that tourists are less likely to return to testify against them should they be apprehended. In other cases, tourist demands for particular goods or services can lead to an increase in criminal activity. This is true, for example, when tourists seek access to prohibited substances, such as drugs or alcohol, or when they engage local people in illegal activities, such as the black market or prostitution.

Tourism can have social consequences in less direct ways. In the United States, for example, the relatively low pay associated with many hospitality jobs has resulted in a tendency for these jobs to be taken by recent immigrants from other countries. The placing of individuals of several different ethnic and national backgrounds into a common workplace has led in many cases to a variety of class, religious, and gender conflicts. Management assumptions regarding cultural compatibility can go awry in such cases. Journalist Kirsten Downey Grimsley (1999) has noted a case in which a major hotel in the United States appointed a Vietnamese-speaking Cambodian woman as the supervisor of a mostly Vietnamese staff. The hotel manager assumed that the woman's familiarity with the Vietnamese language would enable her to work well with her subordinates. Only later, when serious difficulties became apparent, was it discovered that the supervisor's entire family had been killed by Vietnamese soldiers when that country occupied Cambodia.

TOURISM AND GENDER

Gender is an important characteristic of social relations, and its association with tourism can be explored in several ways. One of these is to consider the extent to which the acts of travel and tourism are themselves gendered. A number of scholars have, for example, argued that modern tourism finds its roots in masculine ideals of the travel experience. For Mary Louise Pratt (1992), the traveler's "eye" is an extension of a masculine will to conquer and control, and by extension tourism is represented as an effort to collect and possess the experiences and landscapes of other people. One needs only to scan a handful of tourist brochures from almost any part of the world, but especially from "hot and sexy" places like the tropics, to discover that there are merits to this interpretation. Consider how typically women are depicted in the roles of hosts or entertainers and how readily their images meld into those of a region's landscape, becoming a part of that which is different and picturesque about a tourist place.

The gendering of Western travel ideals has clearly been influenced by history. Early European explorations of the world were almost exclusively conducted by men. During much of the lengthy period in which seafaring was the dominant mode of European travel, women were excluded as nonessential, and their presence on ships was often regarded as bad luck. The travel accounts of explorers and sailors blended the exotic with the erotic as male Western travelers encountered the women of the places they visited. Wars have also contributed to the Western travel experience, and these opportunities (if that's the right word in this case) were again reserved largely for men. Before the advent of modern mass tourism, which did not really take off until after the end of World War II, going to battle was the primary means by which young American men experienced other places and, not coincidentally, other women. What we now sometimes call sex tourism surely has deep roots in the Western imagination.

As powerful as these associations are, however, it seems unlikely that they are sufficient to account fully for the development and gendering of modern tourism. As we noted in the first chapter, early modern mass tourism had close associations with religious experience, with the spiritual and physical valuing of re-creation, and with family-oriented excursions. The ways in which modern tourism is gendered vary in respect to different types of travel experiences, as well as in terms of the kinds of places tourists visit. In the West, business travel, which is still dominated by males, might be seen as an extension of the kinds of male-oriented travel experiences discussed above. Most kinds of leisure and recreational tourism seem to have followed a somewhat different pattern, perhaps more easily associated with the pilgrimage as a variety of travel experience that is less exclusive in terms of gender.

The Japanese experience of modern tourism provides an interesting twist to our appreciation of the gendering of touristic activities. Unlike the West, travel was discouraged in Japan before the time of Western incursion. The country remained fairly insular until World War II, and most domestic travel was limited to the kinds of pilgrimage experiences discussed in chapter 1 of this book. With the end of World War II, Japan embarked on a program of rapid modernization that emphasized devotion to work and home and that further discouraged leisure and extended travel. It was not until the 1960s that a modern tourism industry began to take shape in Japan. By "modern" in this sense I mean an industry that not simply facilitates travel, but that also rationalizes the travel experience in ways that encourage more people to think of travel as a desirable if not necessary part of their lives. In *Discourses of the Vanishing*, Marilyn Ivy (1995) has noted that the emergent Japanese tourist industry of the 1960s focused much of its promotional effort on trying to entice young women to travel. Men, it was felt, were either still too busy to have much thought of leisure-time activities or were so bound to social conventions as to resist travel opportunities that were regarded as superfluous. In an interesting reversal of the tendency to view Western tourism as having developed through a "masculine gaze," Ivy argues that Japan's initial tourism promotion campaign assumed that young, unmarried women were the appropriate pacesetters in encouraging greater societal acceptance of leisure travel. They were assumed to be less bound to social conventions, and they would help broaden the travel market because "where women go, men follow."

Studies such as those mentioned above consider the ways in which travel conventions are shaped at least in part by cultural considerations of gender and sexuality. Other studies have focused on the ways in which tourism can affect gender relations in "host" communities. Principal among these have been studies of tourism-related employment. Much of this research indicates that tourism often provides important new sources of employment and income for women. The result can be consequential in societies in which women do not traditionally have independent access to many employment opportunities. On the other hand, the kinds of opportunities available to women are often limited to those types of jobs that are deemed to be culturally appropriate for women, such as the relatively low-paying opportunities associated with domestic service and craft production.

A. Lynn Bolles's (1997) study of women tourism workers in Negril, Jamaica, makes this same point. The women that Bolles interviewed were engaged in ancillary types of tourism employment, such as hair braiding or operating a few tourist cottages, that served to replicate local gender differences in employment opportunity. The women also reported that they had difficulty in juggling their work along with their domestic responsibilities, because they received little or no help on the home front from male partners. On the other hand, the women viewed their tourism employment favorably in that it provided economic opportunities that they might not otherwise have enjoyed.

To date, most anthropological studies of the relationships between tourism employment and gender have focused on the more marginal segments of a society and have been limited by their attention to the "ethnographic present." It would be valuable to trace changes in gender relations among more diverse segments of a society and over longer periods of time. In Thailand, for example, women's employment in tourism-related activities ranges widely, from housekeeping jobs in hotels to the ownership of major travel agencies. Women are prominent figures not only in the low-paying jobs associated with hospitality but also in many of the major tourism business enterprises that have been developed. In this instance, women's access to higher-level careers may be related to Thai attitudes associated with the status of business careers. Upper-class Thai males have traditionally resisted direct involvement in business, leaving relatively more such opportunities open to minorities (most notably Chinese immigrants) and, more recently, to women.

In other instances, the long-term gender consequences of tourism-related employment might vary in relationship to changes in the industry. In a discussion of women's involvement in the Japanese tourism industry, Hiroko Nozama (1995) notes that the rapid growth of Japanese tourism resulted in a labor shortage that permitted women to compete for types of employment that might otherwise have been denied them. Nozama also suggests that increases in the percentage of female travelers has had a positive effect on the types of tourism employment available for women, as well as upon the perception of the midlevel professional tourism workplace as being "women friendly." She goes on to express the hope that success in the tourism industry will lead to increased opportunities for professional Japanese women in other, more traditionally male-dominated industries.

Tourism is both a gendered industry and an often highly eroticized activity. It is gendered in both the ways discussed above—in the images and ideologies of travel that are conveyed by the industry and borne by the tourist and by patterns of gender-related behavior that can be attributed to the host society. Tourism is eroticized to the extent that it embodies sexual imagery and encourages various expressions of sexuality. Such carefully wrought images include the subtle sexuality expressed by the "honeymoon suite," the public eroticism of beachgoing and sunbathing, and the availability of women and men for hire or friendship in many tourist locations. These evoke some of the most intimate occasions of tourism, particularly when they involve sexual relations between tourists and their "hosts." Sexual activity related to travel and tourism can assume a variety of expressions, including hospitality, companionship, prostitution, and rape. Of these, prostitution has been most closely associated with modern tourism, although its manifestations in particular social settings often blends with the other expressions.

The study of phenomena such as tourist-related prostitution is in fact quite complicated, because an activity like prostitution can be realized in many different ways, even in similar cultural instances. In Thailand, for example, prostitution is sometimes recognized, even officially, as a segment of the country's hospitality industry. The most popular and quasi-official euphemism for prostitutes is "service workers." There are also instances in Thailand in which prostitution is clearly associated with acts of rape, particularly as regards traffic in young girls. On the other hand, much of the international sex tourism that occurs in Thailand appears to be motivated in part by a desire on the part of the sex workers to establish more lasting companionships with their clients (e.g., Cohen 1982). Obviously, the social reality of tourism-related prostitution varies from one circumstance to another.

It should be clear that the various topics discussed in this chapter are closely related. Social relations are played out in political contexts and are shaped in many respects by economic considerations. In virtually every case, culture plays a significant role in determining the meaning of social, political, and economic events that might otherwise seem quite similar.

CASE STUDY: TIROL AND RURAL TOURISM

I suggested earlier in this book that one of the difficulties we have in determining the impacts of tourism is the lack of longitudinal studies that could provide us with a greater time perspective. One such contribution can be found in Martha Ward's (1993) ethnography of the alpine regions of Tirol, located on the borderlands of Austria, Germany, and Italy. Ward did not go to Tirol specifically to study tourism, but rather to understand how the people there had adapted over time to this unique mountainous region. Tourism, it turned out, had begun to play a major role in that adaptation.

In fact, over the past several decades, tourism has become the economic mainstay of Tirol. Tourists come for outdoor recreation, principally skiing, as well as to witness the special nature of a place that is thought to maintain many of its alpine traditions. Because the habitable land area is relatively small, population density (including both Tiroleans and tourists) is now among the highest of any other place in Europe. In Ward's opinion, the Tiroleans have adapted relatively well to the advent of tourism in their region. Tourism has helped revive local craft industries and provided an infusion of new wealth into communities that were on the verge of extinction. Much of this successful adaptation has occurred as a result of what Ward refers to as the practice of "participatory hospitality," which is closely associated with the area's history. In effect, Tiroleans have managed to incorporate tourism into existing social and political structures.

Traditionally, the farmstead has been the basic Tirolean social unit. The valleys in which their farms are located are neatly bounded by mountainous terrain, helping maintain the independence of the villages. As a result, villages are relatively free to welcome tourism on their own terms. The social structure of the individual communities, and of the region as a whole, has long been based on egalitarian ideals. A basic principle of political self-governance has remained intact and highly effective for centuries. Because the region is subject to legal restrictions that prohibit the owning of land by foreigners, Tirol has not experienced the degree of second and vacation home construction that is evident in many other popular tourist regions. In many respects, the farmstead remains an important social and economic unit, even though farming is no longer a major source of income for most Tiroleans. About a third of the tourist accommodations in the region are provided in the form of guest rooms that have been provided by farming families.

There are, however, costs associated with tourism in Tirol. Ward notes that tourism is a pervasive force that threatens to consume its product, and Tirol is no exception in this regard. The mass presence of tourists has resulted in increased social and economic stratification, particularly between those who own and operate tourism facilities and those who provide such ancillary services as housekeeping. Local communities are divided as to the future of tourism in their villages. While some favor continued growth of the industry, others argue for greater control and limits. There have been environmental costs as well. Accumulations of salt applied to winter roads and to skiing areas have adversely effected the ecosystem. The centuries-old local towns are not equipped to handle the heavy traffic of supply trucks and tourist buses, and Ward reports that some structures are being literally shaken apart by the constant passing of these vehicles. Some villagers are concerned that their culture is being trivialized and overly commodified in the service of tourism.

Although modern tourism represents a major challenge for Tirol, Ward suggests that this is not a new condition. Tiroleans have faced crises many times in the past. During the sixteenth century, the region experienced a mining boom that opened the region to commerce and resulted in a population surge that could not be sustained when the industry declined. Economic decline and social unrest lead to a Peasant War in 1525. For much of the next three centuries, Tirol remained fairly isolated from the centers of European growth and development, a process that limited economic growth in the area but also contributed to the strengthening of traditions of egalitarianism and independence. The opening of a railroad in 1867 heralded the beginnings of modern tourism. Victorian travelers extolled the Tiroleans as exemplars of their own romanticized pastoral past, helping to create the imagery of a content peasantry that remains an important part of Tirol's modern tourism. Some of this imagined tranquility was threatened, however, during the two world wars, in which Tirol became a battleground for the nationalistic interests of its constituent countries, disrupting the unity of its unique and borderless ethnic identity. Other events of the first half of the twentieth century had a devastating effect on Tirol's economy as well. Farming was no longer adequate to sustain the villages, resulting in a rapid out-migration of youth that threatened the continuity of social life. Tourism served to help reverse this trend and, although Ward does not mention this, might also have helped repair the fractured identities of the place.

The importance of Ward's account is that it enables us to see that tourists are not alone in seeking to recover pieces of the past through tourism. The people who serve as hosts to tourists also view their participation in light of their own interpretations of their history. These interpretations inform their values—in the case of Tirol, deeply held values of communalism and independence. Past experiences with outsiders also affect the ways in which communities adapt to tourism. Specific historical instances might remain long in a people's memories and broadly influence their responses to the present. Ward notes, for example, that Tiroleans are quick to draw parallels to their current situation in regard to mass tourism and their sixteenth-century experience with the boom and subsequent bust of the mining industry. This lesson from their history informs them that tourism is an opportunity that needs to be carefully managed in order to ensure its survival. More recent experiences have also influenced Tiroleans' attitudes toward tourism, particularly to the extent that the industry is seen as having helped rescue the region from the consequences of severe economic decline.

Ward's study is an example of rural tourism, which is a fairly complex subject in its rights. Rural tourism can include such seemingly benign activities as selling local produce at roadside stands, to homestay visits at working farms, to the re-creation of rural spaces in the form of living museums and dude ranches. In the case described above, tourism is sustained not only by the rural nature of Tirol, but perhaps more importantly by its proximity to mountain recreational opportunities. In other cases, lacking such attractions, the rural landscape itself can become a major draw. This is true, for example, of tourism drawn to Lancaster County, Pennsylvania, where Old Order Amish rural life is a major attraction. Roy Buck and Ted Alleman (1979) have noted an especially interesting aspect of tourism drawn to this region. While scholars of tourism often decry the elaborate "staging" and rampant commercialism associated with popular tourist attractions, Buck and Alleman argue that these kinds of barriers to "authentic" tourist contact have actually helped the Amish maintain their distinct culture and patterns of social organization. Prior to the development of a highly commercialized tourist industry, tourists who wished to experience Amish culture had little choice other than to try to establish direct contact with the Amish. Being somewhat reclusive and protective of their privacy, most Amish found these intrusions to be disruptive. The development of an "Amish" tourism has effectively redirected most tourists away from working farm-steads and concentrated them along two major roadways that cater to their interests.

The Tiroleans seem, on the other hand, to be much less reclusive. This has resulted in a completely different approach to rural tourism that includes homestays and opportunities for tourists to participate in local festivals. Part of the difference might be attributed to the experiences of these rural peoples. The Tiroleans appear to have fared best during those historical periods in which they were closely connected with the rest of the world but still able to maintain their independence. The Amish, on the other hand, have a history that includes persecution and self-exile and have maintained their lifeways by guarding against intrusion on the part of outsiders.

Chapter Three

Nature, Tourism, and the Environment

One day I found myself in a jungle in Borneo. I arrived there by motorized canoe along with a small party of other tourists. When we first approached the Iban longhouse village that was our destination, we were given some time to relax before beginning our "native tour." Only later did I come to speculate that our relaxation also served to allow our Iban hosts time to get into their traditional dress and prepare to make our visit as authentic as possible. Be that as it may, for my relaxation, I chose to take a swim in the small river that we had used to reach the village. It was a slow-moving, crystal-clear stretch of water, and I swam some distance upriver before rolling onto my back to float downstream. I was shaded by a canopy of tropical rainforest and, as I drifted past the Iban village, I felt myself in a great moment out of time. None of the other tourists were in sight. Despite the easy circumstances that had brought me here, I imagined myself to be a wonderful adventurer, at least momentarily on my own in a place of natural beauty and cultural suspense. Sometime later I was informed of how adventuresome I really had been. The Iban tend to be shy of the river, I was told, because of the risk of being attacked by crocodiles.

My overnight stay with the Iban taught me several things about tourism. On the river journey to the longhouse, our guide had gone out of her way to prepare us for a visit to a truly unique people who, she suggested, continue to live closely with nature. She emphasized the Iban's traditional head-hunting practices and led us into a titillating discussion of how young lovers manage to get together for sex in a community that lives together in a single longhouse. Interestingly enough, our tour group was composed of quite well-educated travelers—some German college students, a Swiss architect and his wife, and a Malaysian businessman who had brought his two children to see "their country." (Sarawak, the part of Borneo we were visiting, is a territory of Malaysia.) Most of us were mildly amused, rather than awed, by the guide's attempts to set the stage for us. It was one of the German students, not the guide, who pointed out the signs of deforestation along our river cruise. And, when we did visit the Iban longhouse and were brought to see a dusty collection of shrunken heads, it was the Swiss architect's wife who pointed out that the Iban had stopped head-hunting long ago. The practice was briefly revived by the British during World War II, who offered the Iban rewards for the heads of Japanese soldiers. This, of course, led us to question the images of Iban savagery that had been so carefully laid out for us by our guide.

The most remarkable event of the visit occurred in the evening, when our tour group was invited to go to the longhouse to watch the Iban dance. The performance was similar to descriptions of longhouse visits written by British colonial officers at the turn of the century. We were all provided with sips of a potent rice wine, and the music and dancing filled the common space of the longhouse. And, just as earlier visitors had described, toward the end of the performance we were all invited to make fools of ourselves by joining the dancers. The only noticeable difference from the earlier travelers' accounts was that, after the dancing, the Iban women rushed back to their private living spaces and returned with a variety of handicrafts, which they spread out on the floor and invited us to buy. There was some awkwardness at that moment, and I think most of us felt a bit disappointed by the abrupt transition from a presumably mutually shared social event to a commercial transaction. On the other hand, the Malaysian businessman's five-year-old son was immune from such disappointment. He wandered freely among the offered goods and almost immediately grabbed up a feather headdress and a small bow and arrow set. The next thing we knew, the boy had donned the headdress and was hopping up and down and whooping like a poorly stereotyped American Indian out of some timeworn cowboy movie. What is remarkable is that the entire longhouse, Iban and tourists alike, burst into fits of laughter that seemed to last forever. It was the closest we had been all night to becoming fully engaged human beings, and this sense of common hilarity was based on the innocent introduction of an element of cultural expression that was totally alien to all of us, but one we all understood. I should note that, for all their "closeness" to nature, the Iban had television sets in their private quarters. To my mind, and despite the best efforts of our guide, this brief escape from normality was the most truly authentic moment of our visit.

We will take up the notion of authenticity in the final chapter of this book. Here, we are concerned with the relationship of tourism to nature and the environment. As was noted in chapter 1, Western tourism has had a close association with the exploration and enjoyment of seemingly natural places. This fascination has contributed over time to both the preservation and decline of environmentally sensitive places.

ENVIRONMENTAL IMPACTS OF TOURISM

Tourism has sometimes been described as a "clean" (i.e., nonpolluting industry), and only recently have we learned that it can also be quite a "dirty" business. Tourism can affect the natural environment of a region in a variety of ways. In general, environmental impacts can result from the specific ways in which tourists use a place, or they can arise simply as a consequence of the increased pressure on a natural environment's carrying capacity with the arrival of more tourists and tourism workers. Countries and regions vary considerably in the extent to which they have developed policies and regulations to protect their natural resources from the potentially harmful effects of tourism and other kinds of development. Negative impacts can be most severe in poorer locales that have become economically dependent on tourism but lack the political, economic, or technical resources to create the types of controls and infrastructure that might protect environmental resources.

In *Tourism and the Environment*, Colin Hunter and Howard Green (1995) have identified a number of major negative impacts to the natural environment that can result from tourism development. Tourism can, for example, contribute to pollution problems through the discharge of sewage and vehicle emissions. The compaction of soils as a result of tourist traffic can lead to surface runoff and erosion. Large-scale tourism development, accompanied by increases in the numbers of visitors to a region, can result in depletion of water resources, and the need to generate increased amounts of energy can lead to a scarcity of fossil fuels. Tourist activities can also contribute to the depletion of wildlife and the destruction of vegetation. Increased litter and some types of tourist facilities can also result in the visual "pollution" of the natural landscape.

In some cases, strains on the natural environment are increased as a result of different lifestyle expectations on the part of tourists. Hunter and Green provide the example of practices concerning water usage in the Caribbean. Heavy and often unsustainable demands on this resource are not only the result of increased numbers of tourists, but are also attributable to the fact that each tourist requires, on the average, three times more water than a local inhabitant. Because natural and human environments are complex systems, depletion of a particular resource can have additional environmental effects. A significant decline in the availability of fresh water can, for example, have important consequences for the flora and fauna of a region, contribute to a decline in agriculture and to increased dependency on imported agricultural goods, as well as lead to political and regional conflicts over water rights.

Many popular tourist recreational activities have significant environmental consequences. Snowmobiles contribute to noise pollution.

Mountain bikes and recreational vehicles damage fauna and can cause severe erosion. The creation of skiing areas has contributed to deforestation of mountainsides, resulting in erosion and increased risk of avalanches. Motorboating contributes to water pollution and bank erosion. Scuba diving and other water recreational activities have resulted in the degradation of coral reefs. Golf is one of the fastest-growing recreational activities around the world. The maintenance of golf courses not only requires the expenditure of vast amounts of water resources but also the use of inordinately high amounts of environmentally harmful fertilizers and pesticides, much more than is generally required for agricultural uses.

The recreational activities of tourists can have added long-term effects on the natural environment to the extent that they influence and alter local recreational styles. In Thailand, for example, the rapid expansion of golf courses to attract international tourists has caught the attention of the nation's elite and middle class, who have begun to take up the sport. This has resulted in the need for even more golfing facilities to meet growing domestic demand.

It can be difficult to generalize the environmental impacts of tourism, because uses of the natural environment vary culturally, and environmental conditions differ from one type of ecosystem to another. The culturally specific nature of environmental impacts is well illustrated in Robert Hitchcock's (1997) report on tourism associated with the Bushmen of the Kalahari Desert region of southern Africa. In this sparse environment, Bushmen hunting-and-gathering activities were disrupted in several ways by tourists. Tourist vehicles destroyed important subsistence plants, contributed to erosion problems, and frightened away game. Limited firewood supplies were increasingly being used to fuel tourist campfires. Some plant species were further threatened by their use in the making of handicrafts for sale to tourists. It is clear that, in reporting to Hitchcock on the ways in which tourism was affecting their environment, the Bushmen had a much different sensitivity toward the uses of their natural resources than did the tourists.

Tourism development can have environmental and human consequences that far exceed the impacts that result from the actual presence of tourists. We might think of some of these as "speculative" effects. When regions become caught up in the promise of tourism as a tool for economic development, land resources are frequently subject to rampant speculation, leading to changes in land use patterns that can have important environmental and social consequences, even if the scale of tourism development that has been envisioned is never realized. Stephen Britton and William Clarke (1987) provide an example in the development of tourism in Jamaica during the 1960s and 1970s. Before experiencing a rapid increase in international tourism, Jamaica had developed its economy primarily on an agricultural base. With a tourist boom that began in the 1960s, Jamaica's economy experienced rapid change. Growth in the tourist sector led to a significant increase in land values. Some land was taken out of agricultural use for the development of tourist resorts, and many agricultural workers left the countryside to seek tourism-related employment. These changes in land use led to an even greater escalation of land speculation. Investors who bought up agricultural land for future tourism development often took it out of productive use while they waited for the opportunity to realize a sizable profit from its resale. Many agriculturalists who did not immediately sell their property held the land in anticipation of even higher future land values. While waiting for the high profits, many of these landholders also reduced or altogether halted agricultural production. This, along with the need to feed increasing numbers of tourists, resulted in increased importation of food and led to rising food costs throughout Jamaica. Unfortunately, it eventually became clear that much more land was being held in speculation than would ever be needed for tourism development. As a result, the boom in land prices was rapidly deflated. The loss of agricultural productivity, rising food costs, and the devaluation of real estate had a severe impact on the local economy and contributed to social and political unrest on the island. Eventually, this unrest led to public confrontations with the government, public riots, and some direct attacks on tourists. When this conflict was publicized abroad, there was a significant decrease in tourist arrivals. Accordingly, both of Jamaica's major industries, agriculture and tourism, were now in decline, contributing to still further economic hardship and political turmoil. It was not the presence of tourists that led to this unhappy state of affairs. It was, rather, the mere anticipation of their arrival in ever greater numbers that led to a dramatic shift in the way many Jamaicans chose to value and use their land resources.

The environmental impacts of tourism are not always negative. Tourism development has also provided support for the preservation and conservation of natural resources, particularly in the setting aside of land reserves that might otherwise be lost to natural or human depletion. We will have an opportunity to consider some of these more positive effects in a subsequent section of this chapter. Weighing the positive and negative environmental consequences of tourism is not particularly easy and, again, very difficult to generalize from one case to another. Consider, for example, the impacts that different kinds of tourism can have on wildlife. Although some impacts, such as hunting, seem rather obvious in that they result in the destruction of animals, there are other much more subtle impacts to consider. Even the impacts of hunting can be ambiguous. Controlled recreational hunting can, for example, actually serve useful environmental purposes.

But only a limited number of tourists shoot wild animals. To other visitors wildlife are sights to be seen (even "collected," as with birdwatching) and experienced, as icons of the natural. Still other tourists inhabit places with little thought of the local fauna or sometimes with a wish to avoid contact of any kind—their images of nature are more closely associated with poison ivy, bugs and snakes, and sundry wild beasts. In any case, tourists' relationships with wild species may be much greater than they imagine. Consider, for example:

— Marine life can be adversely affected by tourism with the destruction of coral reefs and other habitats, or when particular species are singled out as tourist food. In parts of the Caribbean, lobster and conch populations have declined because of overharvesting.

— Increase in beach tourism in Turkey has led to levels of noise and light pollution that threaten the breeding activities of endangered sea turtles.

— On the other hand, the populations of some endangered species such as Indian tigers, African elephants, and American bison have increased as a result of the creation of tourist-oriented preserves.

— The increased popularity of whale watching as a tourist activity has contributed to efforts to ban or limit whale hunting and has been offered as an alternative employment for former whalers. At the same time, accidents caused by tourist boats have injured whales, and it has been suggested that intensive whale watching might result in lowered breeding success.

— In Dominica, a successful campaign to save two species of Amazona parrots from extinction was based in part on their value in promoting nature tourism to the island.

— In many parts of the world, dramatic increases in beach tourism have resulted in the disruption of bird nesting sites and have led to declines in bird populations.

— Parts of several endangered species, such as turtle shells and banned ivory, continue to be sold to tourists and, in some tourism areas, "jungle food" restaurants that offer tourists unique taste treats have included protected species on their menus.

— In some parts of Africa, efforts to curb wild animal poaching by members of local communities have included programs that involve these communities in the comanagement of wildlife resources and tourism facilities.

— The "wildness" of wildlife is sacrificed in many places where interaction between tourists and animals become ritualistic, as it often does in the roadside feeding of some species.

Obviously, the relationships between tourism development and wildlife vary both in terms of specific species' adaptations and the types of tourism involved. Efforts to involve local communities in tourism-related conservation activities are often premised on the idea that such involvement will discourage locals from exploiting wildlife for other purposes. The success of such efforts is likely to depend in part upon the

extent to which tourism involvement truly represents genuinely beneficial and culturally desirable opportunities for local communities. Conflict in the uses of wildlife is not limited to tourism in the developing
world. Similar conflicts have, for example, become commonplace in the
increased tourist use of the United States' parklands and forests, where
local access to natural and wildlife resources might be restricted as a
result of tourism development.

TOURISM TO NATURAL PLACES

Humans have placed themselves both as a part of nature and as
existing apart from nature. Most if not all societies make distinctions
between those things that can be attributed to culture, in that they are
fashioned by humans, and those things that belong to nature and could
be expected to exist in the absence of any human presence. Still, the idea
of nature cannot be freed of its cultural context. While many Western
cultures emphasize human mastery over nature, Eastern cultures tend
to place greater emphasis upon humankind's place within the natural.
Modern Western ideological notions of development as a progressive process lend themselves to technological solutions to both "conserving" and
"improving" nature. Some other cultures focus on a more cyclical notion
of nature and appear to be considerably more tolerant of "natural" processes of decline and recovery. Tourism is one way in which people come
to express their relationships with nature. There are at least four types
of excursions into the natural that might be considered in relation to
tourism. They are what I will call the embedded, the frontier, the nostalgic, and the educational.

The *embedded* tourism experience is well represented by the spirit
quest, traditionally practiced by some Plains Indian societies. Here, the
purpose of travel is to isolate oneself from the human community in
order to acquire an identity from nature, often in the form of an animal
spirit. The idea of surrendering oneself to nature in order to experience
one's own "true nature" is typical of this kind of experience. A modern
version of the embedded can be found in the travel writing of Peter Matthiessen (1987, pp. 44–45):

> The search may begin with a restless feeling, as if one were being
> watched. One turns in all directions and sees nothing. Yet one sens-
> es that there is a source for this deep restlessness; and the path
> that leads there is not a path to a strange place, but the path home.
> ("But you *are* home," cries the Witch of the North. "All you have to
> do is wake up!") The journey is hard, for the secret place *where we
> have always been* is overgrown with thorns and thickets of "ideas,"
> of fears and defenses, prejudices and repressions. The holy grail is

what Zen Buddhists call our own "true nature"; each man is his own savior after all.

The *frontier* experience is typified by relationships in which human mastery over nature is emphasized. This might involve travel to well-known frontier places, such as Alaska or the Brazilian rainforest. Here, much of the emphasis of the tourist encounter is reflective of humankind's tenuous hold over a pervasive natural setting. Other aspects of the frontier tourist experience include activities that relate directly to efforts to demonstrate human conquests over nature, such as recreational hunting and fishing, mountain climbing, and white-water rafting.

Much of modern nature tourism takes the form of a *nostalgic* experience. Humankind's appreciation for the natural is often related to our sense of the distance between ourselves and nature. The further we distance ourselves from nature, the more nostalgic are we likely to become. Nostalgic nature tourism is different from the embedded experience, in that nature is experienced from a "safe" distance, as a unique travel adventure from which the tourist fully expects to return.

Educational experiences related to nature tourism are based on attempts to learn more about particular species of flora or fuana, or about natural places or processes, by experiencing them directly. Visits to zoos and wildlife parks can be included here, to the extent that travelers are genuinely interested in learning more about what they observe. Most of the world's zoos have, for example, attempted to transform themselves from places where visitors come simply to see exotic beasts, more appropriate to nostalgic and frontier-like visitor experiences, into places where visitors have an opportunity to learn about wildlife adaptation in complex ecosystems. Many of the approaches to ecotourism, to be discussed in this chapter, fall within this type of experience.

These various ideal types of nature tourism might conflict in important ways. The local population associated with a natural environment might, for example, be experiencing the place as a frontier. Here, the battle for human survival is uppermost in their minds. On the other hand, tourists and the mediators of tourism experiences might be motivated to transform the same place into a reserve devoted to environmental education, or into a site for nostalgic visits to a "lost" natural heritage. I recall in this respect a conversation I once had with a Costa Rican anthropologist, pertaining to Costa Rica's impressive national park system. He pointed out that many rural Costa Ricans fail to see the significance of these parks in the same way as foreign visitors. They are still in a "frontier" mode, in which the rainforest is seen as place that is both dangerous and threatening to their ability to make a living from the land. They are, in other words, too close to the jungle to be particularly nostalgic about it. Enlisting these peoples' support in attempts to preserve the country's rainforests not only requires providing viable economic alternatives but also trying to convince them to change a dominant cultural view that sees the forest as unfriendly and unsafe and therefore worthy only of conquest.

Nature tourism is of several kinds, as well as of the types mentioned above. It can focus on artificially created sites, such as public or private gardens. It can be centered upon scenic attractions, such as mountains, waterfalls, or beaches. Another variety of nature tourism is directed toward large tracts of land that exist in as near a natural condition as possible—areas that serve to represent a region's habitat before the coming of the industrial age, or sometimes even before human habitation.

Most countries have set aside a part of their land areas for preservation in its natural, or nearly natural, state. There are both aesthetic and practical reasons for doing this. The rapid depletion of the world's forests and other habitats has led to serious environmental problems, as well as to a decline in the livelihood of people who have traditionally lived in these areas. These problems often affect a country as a whole. In Thailand, for example, environmental scientists have noted that rapid loss of forest cover has contributed to serious flooding and erosion in many other parts of the country. It has also been recognized that standing forests continue to serve as an important source of food and building material for Thai farmers and tribal groups who live near these areas.

These natural reserves have in many cases become popular tourist destinations. Although there is a potential for tourism to contribute to the degradation of reserves through overuse, many advocates have argued that tourism is a good way to draw attention to natural areas, to protect them from more damaging types of encroachment, and in some cases to provide funds for further preservation efforts.

A number of studies from around the world indicate both the strengths and limitations of nature tourism. In some African states, for example, nature tourism has become a major source of tourism revenue. In part, the current popularity of nature tourism in Africa is reinforced by the past popularity of big game safaris, but in present times the emphasis is often on "bagging" animals with binoculars and cameras rather than with rifles. The African experience indicates that nature tourism is not the exclusive domain of young, low-budget natural history enthusiasts. Most tourists to the continent's popular game reserves mount their expeditions from the comfort of first-class tourist accommodations. Some observers have suggested that a major problem with nature tourism in Africa is that local populations are often displaced as a result of designating large pieces of land as reserves. This is true, and it is a major problem in other parts of the world as well. On the other hand, the relationship between these displacements and tourism is not at all that clear, because the reserves were not designated principally as tourist places, but as environmental protection zones. The question of how effective many reserves actually are in terms of protecting the environment, and whether they are always worth the effort in terms of the costs of displacing local populations, is another matter and needs to be explored on a case-by-case basis.

Nature tourism sometimes involves local, indigenous culture as a part of its object. Edward Bruner and Barbara Kirshenblatt-Gimblett (1995) provide an instance in which a nostalgic approach to nature serves to replicate real or imagined colonial relationships between Western tourists and Maasai tribespeople in East Africa. Here, Maasai participants perform aspects of their traditional culture in the setting of a lawn party held at a former colonial ranch, reproducing, in the authors' terms, relationships between a "genteel British" audience and a "savage/pastoral" Maasai presence. In this case, the performance was staged as a tourist attraction by the British ranch owners.

Some people have opposed nature tourism because they feel it represents a threat to wildlife, especially to endangered species. We have noted several such instances in the preceding section of the chapter. On the other hand, in India's Ranthamhor National Park, the endangered tiger population increased by three times its original number after the park was established. In Rwanda, researchers and animal rights activists originally opposed opening the country's gorilla reserves to tourism. Later, three gorilla "communities" were established—one for research purposes, one to be left as wild as possible, and the other to be available for tourist visits. Some years later, the gorilla population visited by tourists was found to be the healthiest of the three groups. In many areas, tourism developed around endangered wildlife populations has helped reduce the incidence of illegal poaching, although in other cases poaching has actually increased. This may be a result of increased impoverishment of the local population, or in response to international market demands for particular animal parts, such as ivory, tiger penises, and bear gall bladders.

One major problem associated with nature tourism has to do with providing the infrastructure necessary to enable tourists to visit natural areas. Initial attempts by the Kuna Indians to develop nature tourism on their reserve on the east coast of Panama failed because access to the area was too difficult for most tourists. The other side of this problem has to do with controlling the density of tourists once access and accommodations are provided. This has become a major issue in countries such as the United States, where national parks and forests have become popular tourist destinations. Since these areas are considered to be the property of the public, it is difficult to deny access to them. Two approaches to controlling density have been: (1) to close some parks, or areas within parks, for part of the year to permit them to "recover"; and (2) to designate some reserves as "wilderness areas," where no roads or facilities are developed, leaving them accessible only to hikers and backpackers. In some highly popular parks, such as Grand Canyon, the park supervisors have begun to develop means to control the amount of vehicular traffic to the most visited areas, sometimes by prohibiting automobiles and providing public transportation to the sites. This initiative is provocative, given the close association between the advent of automobile tourism and of the early development of many the United States's national parks.

The World Wildlife Fund supported an early study of nature tourism in five countries of Central America and South America. Some interesting results of Elizabeth Boo's (1990) study, which have been widely cited in the literature of nature tourism, are:

— Contrary to what might be expected, tourists who visited these countries because they were primarily interested in nature spent considerably more on a daily basis ($264) than did tourists who reported that they were not interested in the country's natural resources ($173).

— Nature tourists tended to travel in groups rather than alone, and the ratio of male to female tourists was nearly equal, whereas there was a much higher percentage of single male tourists among those who indicated little or no interest in nature. There were more first-time visitors among the nature tourists, and they indicated a higher percentage of satisfaction with their visit than did other tourists.

— The study found little evidence of direct harm to the natural areas as a result of tourist visits. On the other hand, the study did express concern as to whether the countries would be able to cope with increased tourist densities. Potential problems included infrastructural deficiencies, inadequate numbers and training of park guards and tourist guides, and the lack of planning for future developments.

— The most negative impacts were those associated with local populations, many of whom had been displaced by the nature reserves or had suffered as a result of new controls placed upon their livelihood. Promises that these people would benefit from employment associated with tourism were generally not fulfilled. Efforts to employ local people as tourist guides did not usually work out.

— The most environmentally sound examples of nature tourism were found to be those reserves and facilities that had been established by private concerns having a special interest in the preservation of natural areas. These operations were also the most successful in training and employing local populations and controlling the leakage of profits by acquiring most of their needs locally.

While noting that ecotourism has been successful in many of the sites she surveyed, Boo suggests that several problems remain to be addressed. There were, for example, few opportunities for tourists to spend money and thereby to support the parks' preservation efforts. Most of the parks had done little to provide opportunities for tourist-oriented environmental education. And, with some exceptions, almost nothing had been done to involve the local population in the planning and management of the parks.

Coastal zones are among the places visited most often by tourists.

The sea and its coasts figure prominently in the human imagination, and relationships to water resources sometimes assume transformative and spiritual dimensions for visitors. Beaches and other coastal areas occupy a complex place in the development of tourism. They have been and continue to serve as places of retreat and relaxation, while in many cases they have also come to represent opportunities for revelry. In many areas of the world, beaches have become distinguished over time into distinct cultural tourist activity zones. Along the United States Atlantic coast, one can find in close proximity to each other beach areas that are devoted to family recreation, others that have earned reputations as "party" beaches, and other beaches devoted to gay and lesbian visitors. Popular beach areas might also develop particular class-based reputations, with some beaches favored by elite visitors and others frequented by working- and middle-class clientele. In many developing countries, shorelines and beaches might also be divided in terms of the nationalities that tend to visit. Locals are quick to recognize the often subtle boundaries and differences between "Italian," "German," and "Japanese" beaches.

The environmental and cultural impacts of beach tourism can be severe, in part because beaches are relatively confined spaces. Competition for the best beaches can easily lead to displacement of local inhabitants and threaten traditional means of livelihood, especially where local communities are dependent on marine resources. In regions where environmental controls are not maintained or enforced, the development of beach resorts often outstrip the capacity of the local infrastructure to support new construction and dramatically increased visitations. This can lead both to a lessening of the quality of life for local inhabitants and to a degradation of the attractiveness of the beach for visitors. In parts of the developing world that still have abundant coastal resources, beach resorts are sometimes subject to a rapid cycle of rise and decline, in which "soiled" and damaged beach areas are abandoned and new beaches are continually developed for tourists. This "slash-and-burn" approach to beach tourism serves both to spread the threat of environmental damage to coastlines and to limit the extent to which local communities can depend upon tourism as a reliable, sustainable resource. Rapid cycles of tourism development and decline make it even more likely that tourism-related employment opportunities will be taken up by transient workers.

Tourists have long been attracted to islands for their beaches and other marine resources as well as for their distinct characters. In Western imagery, the islands of the tropics have close associations with ideals of remoteness, the search for a paradise on earth, and cultural as well as erotic intrigues. Western tourists tend to approach the inhabitants of these places with the mixed attitudes of colonial and racial superiority, fear, and fascination. Tourism planners and developers have long recognized the extent to which many islands can be marketed on the basis of their most striking indigenous cultural elements. The Holiday Inn bar in Sarawak, on the island of Borneo, serves "headhunter" cocktails. In Hawaii, the hula dance and totem-like souvenirs symbolize decades of successful tourism promotion—never mind that many of the entertainers come from the Philippines or that most of the "authentic" souvenirs and handicrafts are manufactured in places like Taiwan. In the Caribbean, tourist appreciation of distinct music styles, such as calypso and reggae, punctuate complex and often racist images of happy, carefree, slightly lascivious, and occasionally dangerous islanders.

Tourism has become the major source of income for many popular island destinations. These opportunities have not come without costs. Many of the environmental problems discussed previously are intensified on small islands. The provision of fresh water and the disposal of tourist-generated garbage and waste water can, for example, become a major problem on islands in which the tourist population might well exceed that of the local population. The leakage of economic benefits out of the local economy is particularly acute in some island regions, such as the Caribbean, which are dependent on foreign transport, multinational hotels, and imported agricultural goods. Regions like the Caribbean that are served primarily by foreign transport systems are vulnerable in another respect. Airlines and steamship companies directly control the numbers of flights and dockings that bring international tourists to an island and are thereby in a position to negotiate hard for economic concessions. In recent years, Caribbean nations have attempted to band together to counter the powerful influence of international carriers, but only with limited success. A couple of popular cruise ship companies have actually bought small islands in the Caribbean and developed them solely as tourist sites.

The management of tourism in some parts of the world can pose special environmental problems. For example, while tourism to the Antarctic landmass does not involve impacts on indigenous communities, because there are none, the environmental impacts on this fragile ecosystem have multiplied with increased tourist interest. Some of these impacts have proven difficult to manage because national sovereignty over the continent remains in dispute (Hall and Johnston 1995).

PEOPLE AS NATURE

Human cultures sometimes measure their progress in terms of the degree to which they have managed to distance themselves from nature. For some, such an opposition might serve as a gauge of how much they have achieved in relation to other, less "advanced," or even more "savage" peoples. Others might use the same measure as an indication of how much they have lost in their increased dependency upon a culture that seems to be driven by technological innovations and ever increasing habits of consumption. In either case, those people who appear to have stayed behind in the march toward "civilization" hold much fascination, and this interest is frequently expressed through tourism. This kind of tourism is often expressed as an opportunity to observe people whose cultures are presumably simpler and closer to nature. Travel brochures advertising tours of such places as the Amazon, southern African game reserves, or the Himalayas regularly juxtapose photographs and descriptions of local flora and fauna with depictions of indigenous people in traditional dress, in effect, naturalizing these subjects for tourist consumption.

Tourism activities of this kind are sometimes referred to as *indigenous tourism*. Valene Smith (1996) has identified four features that tend to accompany indigenous tourism—the four "Hs" of habitat, heritage, history, and handicrafts.

Indigenous tourism often focuses on the relationships between people and their natural *habitats*. Tourism activities of this kind can be beneficial to the extent that they educate tourists and instill a greater appreciation of the range of human-environment adaptations. Indigenous communities who become the models of these adaptations can also benefit in that their traditional subsistence activities are supported through the added incentives of tourist dollars, in much the same way as rural tourism has sometimes made it possible for small-scale farmers to maintain farming practices that would otherwise be unprofitable. On the other hand, tourist interest in indigenous peoples and their habitats might also prove costly in both environmental and human terms. Robert Hitchcock, whose study of tourism among the Kalahari Bushmen was noted earlier, has pointed out that some important plant species have become threatened by the practice of tourists hiring Bushmen to demonstrate how these plants are traditionally harvested. Local communities sometimes come to resent the extent to which tourists and their guides focus on indigenous practices that might, on a global scale, be seen as "simple" or even "backward." The style of interaction between tourists and their local "hosts" can be an important factor in such cases. Though they might bear it with stony silence, local residents readily perceive the often patronizing attitudes of visitors who view themselves as more knowledgeable and sophisticated in the ways of the world.

Indigenous tourism has also focused on other aspects of a people's *heritage*. Again, one benefit to the tourist can be a greater appreciation of cultural diversity, a value that anthropologists can easily applaud. At the same time, brief and superficial presentations of a people's heritage through the kinds of staged events that are typical of many tourist visits can contribute as easily to misunderstanding and stereotyping. In other instances, tourism that is focused on elements of a people's heritage has helped instill among local communities a greater appreciation of their past. Tourism has actually encouraged some communities to attempt to revive and preserve elements of their heritage. On the other hand, tourist events sometimes focus on the most different and sensational aspects of an indigenous people's heritage, reinforcing images of remoteness, peculiarity, or even savagery. This is clear, for example, in organized tours of the "headhunters" of Borneo or of the "cannibals" of Fiji.

Tourists sometimes engage indigenous societies through an interest in their *history*, particularly in respect to the ways in which these local histories collide with their own. The tourists' interests can be sympathetic. In the United States, for example, tours of former slave plantations afford both black and white visitors the opportunity to improve their understanding of the social and cultural consequences of slavery in light of evidence revealed by recent archaeological and historical research. In other cases, the tourist's interest can be more condescending. Many popular tourist locations in countries that were formerly colonized by Western nations provide visitors with the opportunity to tour some of the architecture of colonialism, if not actually relive the colonial experience. The "lawn party" featuring cultural performances by Maasai tribespersons, mentioned above, is an example of this use of history. Tourist sites that focus on historical relationships between peoples are often the subject of considerable conflict related to their interpretation. We have already noted the extent to which this is true of interpretations of the Israeli site of Masada, as well as of touristic interpretations of the significance of the Alamo. In chapter 4, we will have occasion to review such issues in greater detail.

The relationships between indigenous arts and *handicrafts* and the souvenir demands of tourists can be complex and are often ambiguous. The commercialization of local handicrafts through tourism has sometimes resulted in the loss of the traditional ceremonial or religious value of those objects. In this regard, Smith (1996) points out that the practical needs of tourists can dictate changes in the ways particular handicrafts are produced. Objects might be reduced in size, for example, so that they can fit in a tourist's suitcase. The quality of local arts and crafts can be diminished when these objects are mass produced for tourist consumption and scaled down to appeal to price-conscious visitors. In other instances, tourism has contributed to the revival and survival of important craft traditions, as well as to entirely new craft traditions that have become effectively incorporated in indigenous production. Again, we will have an opportunity to revisit some of these possibilities in greater detail in the final chapter of this book.

To Smith's "four Hs" of indigenous tourism, we might add a fifth "H," that of *healing*. Tourists not infrequently seek out indigenous and "natural" places in search of remedies for their ills. In some instances, this might simply involve trips to particular regions where indigenous medicines and herbs can be obtained. Eric Cohen (1996) notes how Thai tourists have long visited indigenous groups of their country to purchase local healing herbs. In recent years, a kind of "New Age" tourism has developed in the West. The focus in this case is on spiritual quests that imbue certain places and their indigenous populations with mystical and healing qualities. An example would be the popularity of Sedona, Arizona, as a tourist destination. Here, a unique natural landscape has provided the setting for shops that trade in items of Native American symbolism, aromatherapy kits, and healing crystals.

The impacts of tourism on those indigenous people who become the objects of tourist interests vary widely—in respect to the number and particular interests of tourists, the cultural background and hospitality experiences of the indigenous communities, and the larger social and political contexts of which the indigenous communities are a part. The more remote, northern parts of Thailand have long been home to a variety of "hill tribe" people, each with distinct cultures. The number of treks and motorized tours that provide tourists with opportunities to visit these people has increased rapidly. During a 1986 visit to the northern city of Chiang Mai, which serves as the staging point for many of these tours, I counted seven tour companies offering visits to the hill tribes. Four years later, I could count more than forty such enterprises. Advertisements for the tours emphasized opportunities to visit "primitive" peoples still practicing their traditional ways of life, and virtually every company assured potential tourists that their treks would take visitors to remote villages that were not frequented by other tourists. In reality, the tour companies rely on visits to many of the same villages, and tour guides have to time their visits carefully so that the trekkers' illusion of exclusivity will be not marred by multiple groups of tourists visiting the same village at the same time.

While many of Thailand's hill tribe villages have become accustomed to tourist visits and have made their own accommodations to tourism, increased demand and competition has led the tour companies to seek additional and more unique trekking experiences. One direction that this search has taken has been to expand tourism opportunities to groups that are deemed to be more "primitive" than the hill tribes and who might be presumed to be living even closer to nature. Cohen (1996) has described the recent growth of tourism opportunities devoted to visiting Thailand's few remaining hunter-and-gathering peoples. One of these groups, the Mlabri, have remained fairly isolated until recent times. Residing principally as foragers in the forests of northern Thailand, the Mlabri have become marginalized as a result the large-scale destruction of their environment. Cohen notes that most are now dependent upon highly exploitative forms of wage labor, working mainly for neighboring hill tribe villages. Organized tours to visit the Mlabri are usually arranged through hill tribe intermediaries. On these occasions, at least some of the Mlabri appear dressed in traditional G-strings, which they have otherwise abandoned. Their payment for participating in this tourist ritual is a pig, which they slaughter and eat in the presence of the tourists. For many Western tourists, this is a somewhat savage display that serves to further reinforce their sense of the Mlabri's primitive nature. Cohen is somewhat ambiguous as to the possible costs and benefits that the Mlabri have derived from tourism. They get a pig for showing up, which is better pay than they are likely to get when they hire their labor out to the hill tribe villagers. On the other hand, they bear whatever costs might be associated in their minds with having become a spectacle in the eyes of others. Cohen notes that this spectacular staging of the Mlabri is not limited to tours organized for Western tourists. He describes one instance in which several Mlabri were brought to Bangkok to be put on display for the Thai patrons of a department store.

The popularity of indigenous tourism in northern Thailand has encouraged other regions of the country to develop similar opportunities. Tourism promoters in the south of the country have, for example, begun to offer tours that focus on the Moken, a "sea gypsy" people residing on the coasts of the Andaman Sea. Like the Mlabri, the Moken live a precarious existence, and much of their traditional access to the sea has eroded as a result of the rapid expansion of tourism facilities and nature reserves. Efforts to transform the Moken into a tourist attraction have had mixed results. Cohen reports that tourists are frequently disappointed to find that these people, who have been depicted in tourist brochures as "free-roaming, primitive boat dwellers," are actually now living in poverty-ridden shanty towns. Interaction between tourists and the Moken is limited almost exclusively to casual sightseeing. Actual tourism facilities, such as souvenir and food stands, are operated by outsiders. The only direct benefits the Moken appear to derive from the tour buses that enter their community are the coins that children are able to beg from the visitors.

The kinds of tourism experiences described above are among the most extreme in terms of human encounters. They bring in close proximity people with widely divergent life opportunities and as a rule provide little if any opportunity for genuine social exchange. While the promotion of such tours often emphasizes the persistence of traditional and "natural" lifeways, the insightful visitor is likely to find in them little else than a death tour depicting the final stages of the destruction of a people. The "host" communities are often thoroughly marginalized within the countries in which they reside, and tourism developers frequently call upon their services and demand their cooperation using the same exploitative practices that have otherwise been employed to deprive them of the opportunity to maintain their traditional livelihoods or to advance in the larger society. While some tourism scholars have expressed a concern that tourism itself might contribute to an erosion of the traditional lifeways of these vulnerable people, in most cases this has already been accomplished as a result of earlier and more devastating intrusions.

There are other instances in which indigenous tourism does not seem nearly so compromising of the local community. John Caslake (1993) has described tourism to Iban longhouses in Borneo. He reports that the Iban tend to view the experience in a positive light, not only because they profit from the visits but also because they genuinely enjoy their encounters with tourists. In this case, one factor might be that the visits are relatively short and infrequent, permitting the Iban to carry on their normal activities without having to endure a constant stream of visitors. In a study of tourism to aboriginal communities in Canada, Valda Blundell (1995) notes that some Indian villages have taken the initiative in tourism development. In these cases, tourism not only provides added revenue but also helps the village achieve greater control over the ways in which their cultures are represented. Tourism is used by some of these villages as a means of demonstrating that they have a history rather than just a "traditional" past. It also provides an opportunity for the villagers to present concerns they have in regard to their treatment by the Canadian government to a wider, international audience.

Modern tourism has served to reinforce Western ideals that associate some people with "nature" and others with "civilization." These associations can be quite exploitative, but in other cases they have provided communities with important and financially rewarding links to the outside. As we have noted elsewhere, a major factor contributing to a beneficial relationship appears to be the degree to which a tourist-receiving community has the ability to control its interactions with tourists and tourism mediators.

ECOTOURISM

Competition within the tourism industry has led to increased segmentation of its market. Rather than promoting a limited range of travel opportunities to tourists, promoters and travel agents have begun to recognize the value of catering to increasingly specialized travel "niches." New markets have developed around the special needs and interests of older travelers, handicapped tourists, gay and lesbian tourists, and particular ethnic groups. Tourism development has also shown increased segmentation in terms of the types of tourism that are promoted. Mass tourism has begun to be augmented with various kinds of "alternative" travel opportunities, such as adventure tourism, which often focuses on "extreme" travel adventures and recreational activities, and ecotourism, which facilitates travelers' interests in the natural environment. The popularity of venues such as ecotourism is a result both of tourist demand and of the travel industry's increased interest in developing and encouraging this kind of travel experience. Influential tourism mediators, such as the World Tourism Organization, have played major roles in encouraging government agencies and tourism planners to consider ecotourism as a lucrative and sustainable new industry.

As we have seen elsewhere in this chapter, nature tourism and ecotourism have also been encouraged as incentives for the preservation of natural resources. Tourists cannot be attracted to a region's natural environments if those resources have been depleted to the point of extinction. Local communities that once depended on the exploitation of increasingly scarce forest and marine resources might be encouraged to help preserve those resources if they can realize new economic benefits from tourism. The ideal of *sustainability* is the assurance that a resource can be put to human use without threatening its ability to replenish itself. Ecotourism not only encourages the retention and conservation of natural resources but can also serve to educate both tourists and their "host" communities as to the complex interaction of human and natural environments. On the other hand, one of the major problems associated with the recent popularity of ecotourism lies in trying to accommodate increasing numbers of visitors without threatening anew the often fragile environmental resources to which they are attracted. Conversely, another major problem has been the lack of sufficient infrastructure to ensure a reliable flow of tourists. Many ecotourism projects have failed as result of overestimating most tourists' spirit of adventure and failing to provide adequate roads and accommodations for visitors.

The label of ecotourism has come to be applied to a wide variety of experiences, each associated with different strategies and expectations. In some cases, the term is simply used to promote large and complex ecosystems as tourist locations. Entire nations might advertise themselves as havens for ecotourism. The Caribbean island of Dominica has, for example, recently attempted to present itself in its entirety as a place of special natural beauty, unspoiled in part by the comparatively small role that Dominica has played in earlier styles of tourism to the region. Other governments might promote tourism related to particular features of their landscape—the Oregon Coast, for example, the Swiss Alps, or the Serengeti Plain of West Africa. Promotions of this scale may or may not include specific provisions to protect the environmental and human resources that attract tourists. In some cases, as in the development of large tracts of land for forest reserves, ecotourism can serve as an alternative form of development that is meant to protect the resource from more harmful uses, such as logging and mining. In other cases, as in the development of marine reserves, tourism itself might be one of the more deleterious uses of the resource, and rigorous controls might be needed to protect the resource from tourist activities.

In most instances, large tracts of land and sea that are set aside for preservation and for the development of ecotourism have been subject to prior uses by local inhabitants. Nearby communities that once had unchallenged access to the resource sometimes find their activities limited if not prohibited as these areas come under greater government control. Locals might find themselves in direct competition with tourists for such resources as hunting and fishing grounds, grazing rights, spiritual sites, and the solitude associated with wilderness areas. David Weaver (1998) has applied the label PCPD (popular, casual, passive, diversionary) to the kind of ecotourism that is generally facilitated by this approach. The aim of this more passive approach to ecotourism is simply to accommodate tourists without causing environmental harm to a resource. More active styles of ecotourism have a "transformational" character. Their aim is to promote environmentally related lifestyle changes among tourists and to encourage uses that actively contribute to the well-being of the natural resource.

In his assessment of the more passive approach to ecotourism in Kenya's national parks, Weaver notes two major problems. One is that park planners have been unable to control the concentration of visitors to a relatively small number of parks and sites within the system, resulting in overcrowding. The other problem is the alienation of local communities, which Weaver attributes to a perception held by many Kenyans that the entire national park system is a part of their colonial legacy. Even with independence, some Kenyans feel that the parks serve mainly the interests of foreign visitors and national elites, providing little benefit to local populations.

The more active approach to ecotourism is usually of a smaller scale and might be directed to just one or a few resources. In south-central Mexico, for example, recently established reserves for migrating monarch butterflies have been opened for ecotourism, in part to encourage local landowners to voluntarily stop legal and illegal logging activities by offering them an alternative source of income. Paul Forestell (1993) offers another example related to whale watching off the coasts of Hawaii. Here, the emphasis is upon changing tourists' attitudes toward whales in particular and toward the environment in general. The aim of the program is to shift the tourists' focus from whale sighting and species identification toward encouraging a greater understanding of the place of whales in the ecosystem. The whale watching trips begin with a focus on whale behavior and conclude with a more general discussion of local and global environmental issues, encouraging tourists to become more actively involved in conservation efforts in their own communities.

A third type to ecotourism, which generally includes elements of the more "active" approach described above, is distinguished by its attention to the needs and concerns of the local communities where tourism occurs. In some cases, visits to the local population might be a part of the tourist experience, focusing again on the relationships of the people to their natural environment. In Australia, for example, there is growing pressure to involve Aboriginals directly in tourism activities that impinge upon their cultural and natural resources. W. E. Boyd and G. K. Ward (1993) have suggested that this involvement should not only include opportunities to realize economic gain from tourism but also allow for Aboriginals to play decisive roles in the selection, development, and promotion of tourist sites.

Other approaches to ecotourism focus less on making the indigenous community a part of the tourism experience and more on using ecotourism as a means for local economic development. An example is the Santa Elena Rainforest project, begun in Costa Rica in 1990 (Wearing and Larsen 1996). The Santa Elena project was started in a forest reserve that had been acquired by the local high school, with the purposes of providing the school with added financial resources, addressing local environmental problems associated with deforestation, and providing employment opportunities for students and other members of the community. In their evaluation of the project, Wearing and Larsen note that the effort was successful on several counts. The reserve was hosting more than 7,000 visitors by 1993, compared to a local population of approximately 3,000 citizens. The local high school had expanded its curriculum to include new courses in English, hospitality, and biology. This expanded curriculum and opportunities to gain experience in ecotourism by working at the reserve had already proven helpful in preparing students for related kinds of tourism employment in other parts of the country.

Despite these successes, Wearing and Larsen (1996) note that some of the general goals of ecotourism had not been accomplished at Santa Elena. The local community seemed much less appreciative of the benefits of the project than might have been expected—in part because few perceived it as specifically benefiting themselves, and few understood the benefits that accrued to the high school and some of its students. The residents of Santa Elena cited several negative impacts of tourism into their region. These impacts ranged from an increase in drug and alcohol abuse, a perceived negative influence on the youth involved in the project, increases in the cost of living, and a loss of tranquility and security associated with the large numbers of tourists and the "party" atmosphere associated with their visits. In some respects, Santa Elena had become a victim of its success. Many of the unanticipated consequences associated with the project were a result of inappropriate social and cultural behaviors on the part of tourists. An assumption that visitors who seek ecotourism experiences might be more culturally sensitive than other kinds of tourists did not seem to hold true in this case. Wearing and Larsen (1996) have suggested that the project's focus should be expanded from that of environmental education to include sociocultural education, with programs developed to inform visitors of the importance of honoring local community standards as faithfully as they might value the natural environment.

The increased popularity of ecotourism is sometimes associated with what has been called the "new tourism." Features of this new tourism include the search for alternatives to resort-centered, mass tourism, with an emphasis on unique travel adventures and sustainable tourism activities. Just as the term *ecotourism* has been used to describe a considerable variety of touristic activities, the concept of sustainability is also subject to several usages. For some, sustainable tourism refers to not much more than the principle of avoiding harm to the environment, something akin to the backpacker's admonition to "pack it in and carry it out." For others, sustainability is associated with more complex interactions between humans and the natural and built environments. In this vein, Cheryl Little (1996) has identified five interrelated principles of sustainable development. They are the appropriate use of technology, ecological preservation, social justice, democracy, and aesthetic harmony. Although Little was interested solely in the sustainability of modern transportation systems, the principles she offers apply equally well to tourism.

As an example of the *inappropriate use of technology*, we might note the extent to which tourism in the United States relies on the use of privately owned vehicles. Automobiles are not only inefficient uses of energy, but their use to transport tourists from place to place results in added noise pollution, congestion, and increased harm to the environment related to road building and the provision of parking areas. In this respect, the tourist-related transportation strategies of many lesser-developed countries are clearly superior. In these places, tourism has not developed in such close association with automobiles, and many such countries have created systems of mass or alternative transportation that result in considerably less strain on the environment and on precious energy supplies.

The goal of *ecological preservation* can be related to efforts to protect the natural environment from inappropriate tourist activities and from the results of overcrowding. Many of the efforts discussed elsewhere in this chapter fall in this category. It is worth noting that it has been only over the past decade or so that many of the environmental hazards of tourism have begun to be recognized. Sustainability in this respect seems much more difficult in parts of the world where the need for tourist generated income is greatest and where local environmental controls are lacking.

Little's principle (1996) of *social justice* aims to ensure that the benefits and costs of tourism are realized in an equitable fashion. We have seen that this is not always the case. In fact, the unequal distribution of benefits is likely to be closer to the norm. Ideals of social justice are in jeopardy when public money that is invested in tourism developments benefits elite investors at the expense of others, or in cases in which the funds might be better spent to encourage other industries or be used for the provision of public services, such as education. Other threats to social justice occur in instances in which especially vulnerable segments of a population are displaced or are subject to higher costs as a result of tourism, without having been afforded much opportunity to benefit directly from the activity.

Little's ideal of *democracy* pertains to the amount of control people have over decisions that are made concerning their communities. The decision whether to encourage tourism in an area, the types of tourism to be encouraged, and how the benefits are to be distributed within a community are all matters over which a local population may or may not have much control. This can also apply to rules of behavior regarding interaction with tourists, ordinances that prohibit or restrict access to areas frequented by tourists, or new rules that forbid particular subsistence or recreational activities on the part of local community. The extent to which people who are affected by tourism development have any voice at all in helping determine the nature of its development varies widely from one locale to the next.

The principle of *aesthetic harmony* pertains to ways in which tourist activities and facilities relate to their surroundings and, in Little's terms, to the "unique identity of place and nature" of a location. Such elements might apply to the built environment as well as to the natural environment. A high-rise tourist hotel that looms above a nearby town's traditional, two-story architecture creates anomalies of scale and presentation that render the original landscape unsustainable. The mere presence of tourists in large numbers can subvert a place's identity, particularly in instances in which that identity is associated with physical isolation or undisturbed natural resources. In other cases, of course, hordes of tourists *create* a place's identity, as they do on the French Riviera and at other popular beach resorts.

Laudable as these ideals of sustainability are, we need to keep in mind that they are also subject to varied cultural interpretations. Not every people holds the same sense of "aesthetic harmony" or interprets issues of democracy or social justice in the same way. Even ideas of what is or is not "natural" and worthy of preservation vary considerably, and people hold strikingly different interpretations and cultural values related to their relationships with the environment. The struggle to define and agree upon the terms of sustainability across cultures can be a difficult one, especially since most of the recent "environmental ethic" that has informed the struggle for sustainability has developed in relation to Western values and experience.

Some observers have noted that the different principles of ecotourism are seldomly applied equally. For example, George Hughes (1995) has argued that rationalist Western approaches to sustainability have favored "scientific" approaches that rely on technological solutions. Considerably less attention has been paid to the human dimensions of ecotourism. In some instances, for example, "community participation" can involve little more than simply informing the local community of the development and seeking their compliance. Hughes suggests that a truly sustainable approach to tourism will require winning over the "hearts" as well as the "minds" of the local population. That is possible only if communities are allowed the opportunity to play a decisive role in determining the scope and variety of tourism developments.

In the context of ecotourism, principles of sustainability often have been applied only to relatively small-scale enterprises, in which the number of visitors to an area are limited (e.g., Honey 1999). As laudable as such efforts might be in serving to protect particular fragile resources and serve the interest of some communities, they manage less well to protect complex ecosystems. While we might allow that "small is beautiful," it is not always better, and tourism will never be a truly "clean" industry until we learn to apply ideals of sustainability to a broader spectrum of tourism initiatives.

CASE STUDY: ECOTOURISM IN BELIZE

The Central American country of Belize lies just below the Yucatán Peninsula on the Caribbean coast. In recent years, the country has been noted as a major site of ecotourism development, aided in this respect by its large and diversified forest reserves, Mayan archaeological sites, and the second-largest barrier reef in the world. Belize's proximity to the United States, relativity small population, and political stability has added to the country's appeal. In contrast to places like the southwestern United States and Europe's Tirol region, Belize could be said to be in a formative stage of tourism development. Barely 10,000 tourists visited Belize in 1960. Thirty years later, the country reported more than half a million visitors, or about five tourists for every two residents. In 1984, tourism revenue represented approximately 7.6 percent of the country's gross domestic product. Only eight years later, it accounted for more than half of the gross domestic product (Woods, Perry, and Steagall 1994). Much, although not all, of this growth is attributable to Belize's reputation as a place for ecotourism. The variety of ecotourism opportunities is diverse, ranging from marine facilities on the coast to jungle preserves that focus on the preservation of particular flora and fauna, to other programs that facilitate visits to indigenous communities.

One of Belize's first ecotourism sites was started in 1984 by two biological scientists from the United States. Robert Horwich and Jon Lyon (1993) began at that time to work with local farmers to establish a "baboon" (the creole term for howler monkeys) sanctuary along the Belize River. The success of the project depended on being able to convince the farmers to adjust their shifting agricultural practices in such a way as to preserve the monkey's habitat. In return, the farmers were offered a stake in the sanctuary's potential for generating tourism revenues. Local farmers currently serve as tourist guides and provide accommodations for visitors. Importantly, this ecotourism project was developed in such a way as to allow the farmers to continue their agricultural practices, making tourism an added bonus rather than a substitute for their more traditional subsistence activities. The sanctuary has enjoyed a broad base of community support and, in part because of its close proximity to Belize City, has generated sufficient interest on the part of tourists.

Another ecotourism site, the Toledo Ecotourism Project, was established by a consortium of five Mayan villages, with the assistance of an expatriate from the United States. More remote than the baboon sanctuary, the Toledo project offers visitors the opportunity to stay in guesthouses constructed in each of the villages. Tourists are guided on forest walks, fed local creole cuisine, treated to dance performances, and offered handicrafts for purchase. The money received from tourist overnight stays is paid directly to a community association. Although judged to be a success, the project is limited to some extent by its inaccessibility—which in the long run might, of course, prove to be a blessing.

Both of the above examples of ecotourism have been described in an article by J. M. Edington and M. A. Edington (1997). In comparing the two projects, the authors note that the baboon sanctuary has the advantage of a clear conservation goal and a well-developed interpretation program. The aims of the Toledo project, which seem less clear to the authors, rest primarily on an assumption that increased revenue from tourism will reduce the villagers' need to clear additional forestland for agricultural purposes.

Many of the ecotourism initiatives in Belize were begun with the support of outsiders. An ecotourism project on Belize's coast has been established on the site of a biological station once operated by a Massachusetts-based environmental institute (Kanga, Shave, and Shave 1995). The Possum Point Biological Station focuses on bringing small and selected groups of visitors (typically high school and college students and naturalist groups) from the United States for extended stays. Eco-tourism opportunities include both marine and forest environments, al-though there is less of a "cultural" component than is apparent at the sites mentioned above. Still, it has been estimated that about 80 percent of the tourism-generated revenue is returned directly to the local community. Visitors, many of whom are themselves students, also have contributed to a fund to provide educational opportunities for local youth. This is an interesting model, in that the goal of many other ecotourism projects is to provide local communities with the resources necessary to maintain their "traditional" lifeways. The Possum Point model provides support for local youth who have their sights set on other horizons. In this respect, there are similarities with the previously discussed

Santa Elena Project in Costa Rica, where most of the revenues from ecotourism were used to support the local high school.

These are only a few of a fairly extensive network of ecotourism
opportunities that have developed in Belize during the past 15 years or
so. Several of these activities are supported by an infusion of foreign capital that is provided by international conservation agencies, such as the
World Wildlife Fund and the Nature Conservancy. Even visitors who do
not come to Belize principally as ecotourists support environmental and
preservation efforts by paying an airport tax that is designated for these
purposes (Honey 1999).

The success of Belize's ecotourism industry has not come without
costs. Many of the tourists who visit ecotourism sites still do so from the
luxury of resort-style hotels built along the country's coastline and in
Belize City. The rapid growth of these facilities has resulted in strains on
the region's infrastructure and coastal environment. Compared to some
other countries, Belize has done little to discourage foreign ownership of
its land and tourism facilities. Nancy Lundgren (1993) has pointed out
that approximately 70 to 90 percent of the country's freehold land is
owned by foreigners. Sixty-five percent of the members of the Belize
Tourism Association are foreigners (McMinn and Carter 1998). For the
majority of Belize's women, tourism has offered little benefit other than
low-paying employment opportunities in hotels and other facilities
(McClaurin 1996).

Ecotourism does not necessarily fail on these counts. Belize's recent
experience with ecotourism provide many genuine successes in environmental protection and local community involvement. Other countries
have suffered the same and even more serious consequences of tourism
without the added benefits associated with effectively managed ecotourism. All the same, this case does inform us as to how important it is to
consider even the most laudable tourism aims within a larger context of
international and regional development and with an eye toward better
anticipating the consequences of any tourism initiative.

Chapter Four

Tourism and Culture

Several years ago, while I was attending an anthropological conference in Memphis, Tennessee, a colleague and I decided to visit the city's new Civil Rights Museum. The museum has been built alongside the Lorraine Motel, where the Reverend Martin Luther King, Jr., was assassinated in 1968. Because it is a part of this story, I need to note that my colleague is a black woman, and I am white. The museum was supposed to be close to our hotel, so we decided to walk. Not knowing our way around town, we were soon enough lost, and I stepped into a local bar to ask for directions while my friend waited outside. It was not a classy bar, and the clientele, who were all white, looked more like regulars than tourists. I asked the bartender for directions to the Civil Rights Museum. He shook his head and said he did not know what that was. I asked him if he knew where the Martin Luther King museum was. This time he asked down the bar, "Anyone here know where this King Museum is?" Heads shook "no," and a couple of the guys smiled. Meanwhile, out on the street, my friend asked someone else who told her that the museum was just around the corner and down a couple of blocks.

As we continued our walk, my friend and I speculated as to the intent of the bar's occupants. It was hard to imagine that they really did not know where the museum was. When we did arrive at the place, we were treated to a remarkable exhibit of the struggle for civil rights in the United States. We exchanged a few comments now and then, but for the most part we were lost in our own observations and memories. Somehow, anything I could think to say seemed trivial. The museum tour ended with a visit to the adjoining Lorraine Motel, where we had the opportunity to enter the room where Reverend King had stayed and then walk out onto the balcony where he was shot. From that vantage, we could see a middle-aged black woman seated across the street. She was surrounded by placards that identified her as a former occupant of the Lorraine Motel who had been forcibly evicted when the museum was constructed. Ironically, she was protesting the violation of what she held to be her own civil rights.

When my friend and I left the museum, we passed through a black neighborhood on our way back to the hotel. One man greeted us and followed along playing his harmonica, hoping no doubt for some tangible display of our appreciation. A few other black men on the other side of the street noted my friend and me walking together and shouted after us.

"Oreo," they called. "Oreo cookie."

This story serves to point out that tourism is rarely the neatly bounded experience that planners and developers would have it be. Tourist attractions are situated in a world of places and spaces that have to be passed through and that become a part of the tourism experience. Some aspects of that experience can be intensely personal and idiosyncratic. There are relatively few Disney Worlds in the lexicon of tourism places. They are the exceptions rather than the rule, and even these carefully construed and managed places are still subject to intrusions of happenstance. Our tour of Memphis's Civil Rights Museum included encounters with living examples of racism and race-based animosity, as well as a poignant example of the human costs of even the most well-intended tourism attractions. The experience would not have been the same without these added parts of our brief journey.

TRADITION, AUTHENTICITY, AND MODERNITY

In the first chapter of this book, we considered the extent to which tourism practices and ideologies are informed by two major conditions that are often associated with modernity. One is the rise of capitalist economies, leading among other things to an ever expanding reach of *commodification*—a process whereby goods and services that were once considered to be outside the realm of direct economic value and exchange are transformed into commodities that can be bought and sold. Modern tourism provides many examples of this process. Beach and park areas that were once free to visitors and local residents alike can now only be accessed by paying a fee. Among the most rapidly growing commodities associated with modern tourism are those of culture and heritage. The marketing of indigenous arts and crafts, of local performances and festivals, and of places and sites associated with a people's heritage has grown rapidly to become a major segment of the tourism industry.

The second condition often associated with modern tourism is that of *reason*, linked in the Western imagination to Enlightenment values associated with scientific rationality. As we noted, the apparent rise of leisure travel during the late nineteenth century was accompanied by a need to rationalize tourism in new ways. Travel, once primarily associated with risk and onerous activity, was transformed into something that was good for us—healthy, spiritually rewarding, and supportive of the rise and spread of "civilization." The modernization of tourism also required that principles of reason be applied to the objects of travel. Revised orders of time, space, and destiny that were appropriate to the newly discovered "laws" of nature and human behavior had to be invented. The nation-state, dedicated to progress and reason, emerged as a dominant force in the shaping of a modern consciousness. Tourists were encouraged to travel in order to experience, and just as certainly to validate, their own sense of nation. They were also invited to indulge their curiosity through visits to other nations, an activity that could serve as well to reaffirm their own national identities. Worldwide, emergent nationalist ideologies have embraced the principles of progress and struggled to command the loyalties of the varied peoples under their authority. And, as we will see in this chapter, many of these nations have increasingly discovered in the tourist's "gaze" new ways of envisioning and justifying their inventions of nationalist traditions and culture.

As Dean MacCannell (1989) has noted, tourism not only serves as a product of modernity but also performs significantly in contrast to the values implicit to a "modern" view of life, particularly in its devotion to ideals of tradition and authenticity. In MacCannell's view, modern tourism has come to embody a reaction against the constraints and ideology of the modern condition. It is a leisured search for other traditions that are untouched by modern influences and a longing for a sense of authenticity through which the tourist might at least briefly escape the alienation of the industrial age. Paradoxically, the search is itself an expression of the modernity from which the tourist seeks to escape. In this sense, the attachment of the label *traditional* to particular objects, places, and people serves to establish the pervasive influence of modernity by imagining those few objects of desire that are supposedly not modern.

People whose reality is perceived as traditional by the purveyors of touristic images do not always see themselves in these same terms, at least not until the experience of tourism catches up with them and encourages them to do so. In an often cited essay pertaining to the commodification of tourism in the Basque village of Fuenterrabia, Davydd Greenwood (1989) describes the transformation of a local festival into a tourist event. The Alarde festival commemorates a seventeenth-century Basque victory over the French. It has, however, served the community as more than a marker of a historical event. Greenwood points out that another more significant function of the Alarde is to provide a means for emphasizing village solidarity and celebrating Basque identity. Much of this contemporary meaning was lost, however, when municipal authorities began, with the support of the Spanish government, to promote the Alarde as a tourist event. When this occurred, the festival was transformed from an important community ritual into a public spectacle of "local color." Many villagers lost interest in the festival, and in later years it became an occasion for political tension.

Regina Bendix's (1989) account of tourism in the Swiss village of Interlaken provides a counterexample to Greenwood's study. Interlaken is the site of several major festivals, many of which draw considerable numbers of tourists. Bendix found little evidence of local animosity toward tourism and not much conflict between the private, local uses of community festivals and their more public, tourist-oriented functions. She notes that, despite the presence of large numbers of outside spectators, the villagers continued to be engaged actively in using festival performances as a means asserting and reaffirming their local identity.

There are a lot of unfilled spaces between Greenwood's and Bendix's accounts, and only by attempting to fill some of them can we hope to begin to sort out some of the cultural consequences of tourism. It is worth noting, for example, that the Swiss village, which is a famed site for outdoor recreation, has a long history of tourist development, whereas the introduction of tourism into the Basque village appears to have been a relatively recent event. Tourism is, therefore, fully incorporated as a part of Interlaken's socioeconomic system, whereas in Fuenterrabia the possible benefits of tourism are likely to be less fully realized by the villagers. The two cases also derive from quite different political contexts. Although Greenwood does not provide detail in this regard, it is worth noting that the events he describes occurred during the 1960s, which was a period of intense nationalization within Spain, evoked by the Franco government's aim to unify the country culturally as well as politically. The Basques, often noted for their cultural and political independence, were not always enthusiastic partners in these goals. It is not difficult to imagine how tourism projects that were encouraged by the national government could be viewed as an unwelcome intrusion upon Basque identities. Compared to Spain, conflicts between local and national identities do not seem to be as pervasive in Switzerland. Bendix suggests that the villagers of Interlaken view many festivals in a positive light because they provide evidence of the region's contributions to the nation.

A question posed by these two studies is whether local traditions, such as community festivals, become any less *authentic* when they begin to involve tourists. Our answer depends in part on how we decide to deal with the notions of tradition and authenticity. For example, most Marxist interpretations, such as MacCannell's, presuppose that capitalist ideologies have deprived modern and modernizing peoples from any claim to authenticity, to realness, and ultimately to control over the modes of production that provide them with at least the possibility of autonomous social action. These same approaches assume greater claims to authenticity on the part of precapitalist societies.

Other interpretations have not made such a sharp distinction between capitalist and precapitalist societies, and have focused instead on continuities in the "inventions" of tradition. Eric Hobsbawn and Terence Ranger (1983) argue, for example, that traditions are always invented and continually being reinvented. Their approach centers on the *agency*, or deliberateness, that informs the construction of traditions. Examples of invented traditions associated with tourism abound. The now "traditional" silver-crafting industries of the Mexican town of Taxco were invented during the 1930s with the encouragement of a visitor from the United States. Many Native American basketry, pottery and jewelry-making traditions have evolved as a direct result of tourist and collector preferences for particular styles and types of these crafts. Much of the music and dance associated with Hawaiian tourism performances was borrowed from elsewhere. While some observers might find in these cases evidence of cultural fakery, others are just as likely to argue that the origins of particular traditions are much less significant than is the degree to which they become incorporated into distinct cultural identities.

Richard Handler and Jocelyn Linnekin (1984) have contended that our tendency to judge authenticity in terms of the faithfulness by which traditions are passed intact from one generation to another fails to account for the ways in which traditions actually serve human communities. Traditions, they argue, are invariably defined in the present and reinterpreted to meet the ideological needs of the living. The invention, appropriation, and reconstruction of tradition is not a consequence of modernity, but perhaps more nearly a necessary condition for the construction of all human culture. Modernity and capitalism did not create these mechanisms, although they might have helped speed them up and, in so doing, perhaps made them more transparent. This transparency, which serves to render previously implicit cultural traditions more explicit, makes it increasingly difficult to perceive modern tourist images as being "real." In this respect, Handler (see Handler and Saxon 1988) joins MacCannell in asserting the virtual impossibility of achieving a sense of authenticity in modern times.

Edward Bruner (1999) has accused both MacCannell and Handler of overstating the modern quest for authenticity and of projecting "onto the tourists their own view of themselves." Bruner argues for a "constructivist" interpretation that does not recognize such a radical break between modern and premodern uses of tradition and that does not differentiate so harshly between original representations and their copies. He has applied his approach to an interpretation of the New Salem Historic Site, which is a reconstruction of an Illinois village where Abraham Lincoln once lived. Bruner suggests that a "postmodern" interpretation of the site would emphasize the contrived and inauthentic construction of the site. This is a different view from the perspective he obtained by observing and interviewing the tourists who visited New Salem. Here, the question of authenticity seemed less immediate and was subordinate to the actual uses the tourists made of the site. New Salem became an opportunity for visitors to "construct a sense of identity, meaning, attachment, and stability." Bruner notes that while it remains possible to be pessimistic about the intentions and ideologies that underlie tourist attractions such as New Salem, it is also possible to view them as opportunities for transformation, in which tourists are actively engaged in interpreting the "raw material" of tourism into genuinely experienced parallels to the present as well as positive engagements with the future.

In some cases, the representations made in the name of tourism do not refer to any lived reality. Alan Bryman (1995) makes this point in regard to the Disney theme parks, where many of the amusements and images are self-referential and drawn from the purely fictional experiences of cartoon characters. This is just the opposite of the kind of heritage tourism described by Bruner. While New Salem is a place imaged out of the past, the Disney theme parks are places in which the imaginary is realized and, consequently, made real. Of course, if we follow this logic, then the New Salem Historical Site is real, too, even though it might well misrepresent the past.

Much of our thinking on these matters is shaped by the popular view that traditions arise and prosper from relative degrees of cultural isolation, somewhat in the same manner as biological species develop and assume unique characteristics as a result of adaptation to particular ecological niches. In this view, distinct cultural traditions become threatened when isolation is no longer possible—hence, the importance of having to protect "traditional" and "authentic" societies from the effects of cultural encroachment, including the invasion of tourists. This assumption is problematic, however, and it seems just as likely that distinct, culturally identifying traditions have often developed as a result of processes of differentiation that arise from exchanges between cultures. In this sense, cultural traditions are constructed more from a recognition of difference than they are the result of a lack of exposure to other cultures.

These are important points for our study of some of the cultural impacts of tourism. In what ways does tourism contribute to the maintenance, destruction, or reinvention of a people's traditions? Do so-called traditional societies that are subject to tourism and other acts of modernization lose their authenticity as a result of these relationships, or is that even a relevant question?

We need to ask at this point whether there are any criteria by which we can usefully differentiate the authentic from the inauthentic. From my perspective, any such criteria would have to support the idea that authenticity is possible under the conditions of modernity. I remain unconvinced that the real is a thing of the past, or that the past was at any time more real than the present. Accordingly, my sense of the authentic is that it occurs under conditions in which people have significant control over their affairs, to the extent that they are able to play an active role in determining how changes occur in their social settings. In this view, all cultures are dynamic by their very nature. Resistance to change is as much an act of deliberateness as is the will to adopt new customs and practices. Authentic cultures might not be able to predict their futures or to act in a wholly independent manner, but they have the wherewithal to play a significant role in participating in those processes that will shape their lives. In this respect, a community that has the ability to decide to tear down all its historic buildings in order to construct a golf course for tourists is more authentic than is another community that has been prohibited by higher authorities from doing the same thing in order to preserve the integrity of its past. This might seem like an extreme example, and its outcomes might not be to our liking. All the same, it reflects upon my suggestion that without significant degrees of autonomy, any notion of authenticity is meaningless.

A less jarring example can be found in Betty Duggan's (1997) discussion of the evolution of a North Carolina Cherokee community's arts and crafts traditions. In this case, the decision to develop handicrafts for tourist consumption originally was encouraged by federal government sponsorship and oversight, and the design and production of the craft items has clearly been influenced over the years by tourists' tastes. On the other hand, the Eastern Cherokee have maintained control over the process and have adapted the production and sale of crafts to their cultural values. Duggan notes, for example, that elected officers to the crafts cooperatives remain faithful to the Cherokee ideal of participatory, rather than hierarchical, decision making. The production and marketing of the crafts are also conducted in such a way as to conform to Cherokee values regarding "non-competiveness, respect for elders, and ways for dealing with mutual aid during times of economic and personal distress." The baskets and other crafts offered for sale at the cooperative might not be exactly the same as those produced a century earlier, but the processes by which they have made their way to the tourist market appear to be notably similar. They are, in this sense, closely tied to Cherokee traditions and authentic in their own right.

By linking authenticity to relative degrees of autonomy, I do not imply that communities are always in agreement as to what constitutes authentic representations of their cultural and social lives. Disagreements on such matters are more likely to be the case. The critical point rests with how much opportunity community members have to disagree and try to settle among themselves the terms by which they are represented. Neither do I imply that everything involved in the representation of peoples and communities need be judged authentic just because those people and communities have control over such matters. In some cases, communities involved in the tourist trade knowingly exploit stereotypes of themselves in order to attract tourists.

TOURISM AND ETHNICITY

Whether or not tourism contributes to or detracts from cultural authenticity might depend less on the strict maintenance of particular manifestations or symbols of culture and more on the processes by which culture is continuously negotiated. We can see how such processes operate in relation to different kinds of *ethnic tourism*. In most instances, the term *ethnic tourism* has been used to refer to activities that engage tourists in the experience of cultural events and situations that are distinct from their own. A number of the social consequences of this kind of tourism have been discussed in the preceding chapter. Here, we will focus on some of the more symbolic and referential aspects of ethnicity and tourism, especially as they relate to issues of nationalization and ethnic minorities. In their volume devoted to ethnic tourism in Asia and the Pacific, Michel Picard and Robert Wood (1997) argue that tourism has in particular instances helped further the aims of modern nation-states in their relationships to ethnic minorities within their borders. Tourism has provided incentives for the physical containment and control of minority ethnic groups and provided opportunities to construct cultural representations of minority groups that are compatible with national ideologies. On the other hand, there are instances in which ethnic minorities have managed to use tourism to assert their own unique identities and to differentiate themselves from nationalist imagery, as well as other cases in which minority communities successfully have resisted tourism as being incompatible with their cultural values.

One interesting study regarding the latter possibility that appears in Picard and Wood's volume concerns a Hmong village in northern Thailand. Much of the literature on ethnic tourism focuses on the unequal relations between nations and their minority populations, pointing to the dangers of increased economic dependency upon tourism and to the risk of communities losing their local identity in the face of pressures to identify with national cultural expressions. Jean Michaud's (1997) study of the Hmong village asserts that frequent trekking visits to the village have resulted in a rejection of such activities on the part of village leaders who once participated actively in hosting the trekkers. While some Hmong continue to participate in trekking visits, they are regarded as marginal by other community members. Michaud asserts that the reasons the Hmong leaders have begun to resist tourism include a perception that they cannot be "authentically Hmong" when they are engaged in such activities. Tourism interrupts the cycles of agricultural and lineage-based production that provide the basis for social interaction in the community, and most of the villagers have decided that the benefits of tourism are not worth the costs associated with this disruption.

Hill tribe tourism in northern Thailand is a good example of the rapid growth of ethnic and cultural tourism. Trekking visits to the various hill tribes first became popular among young, adventure-seeking tourists. These included international visitors and urban Thai youth who, among other things, sought access to the ready availability of opium in the region. Currently, visits to the hill tribes have become popular among a greater variety of tourists, with brief coach tours made available for the less adventurous traveler. Some of the negative effects of tourism to the area have been cited by Cohen (1983). They include: (1) increased use and dependency upon drugs, aside from the traditional uses of opium in many villages; (2) increased dependency upon a market economy; and (3) a loss of dignity that comes about as a result of becoming objects of curiosity. There have also been some positive effects that can be attributed at least in part to tourism. For example, tourism does provide a source of supplemental income for villages that have suffered the loss of traditional lands and other sources of income. Tourism has also helped make the hill tribe people more visible to other Thai, who have become increasingly aware of the marginal status of many of hill tribe communities.

It is difficult to determine how much tourism has affected the social and cultural lives of the different hill tribe people. Certainly other factors associated with modernization—such as the establishment of national schools, forced relocation, agricultural development programs, and new road construction—have had a greater impact. Also, the impacts of tourism are likely to vary from one ethnic group to another, depending on cultural and social differences, as well as upon the types of tourism each group is willing to entertain. Northern Thailand's Yao people, for example, seem to have adapted to tourism with a minimal impact upon their community life. Here, tourism is usually centered upon selling arts and crafts to tourists and is simply an extension of the Yao's long-standing experience in trading with other hill tribes and visitors to the region. The impact seems to be greater among the Akha, where trekking tourists often stay overnight. Traditionally, the Akha are shifting agriculturalists, and until recently they have had little experience in accommodating visitors to their villages. In some Akha villages, both increased drug use and prostitution have occurred as a result of tourism. The Akha have also had to adapt to tourist behaviors, which have included routine violations of religious and community standards, and this adaptation has perhaps contributed to a lessening of the strength of local beliefs.

For the most part, Thailand's hill tribe tourism has not been developed for the well-being of the villagers, but for the profit of outside entrepreneurs who operate the tour guide services. In some cases, hill tribe villages have become dependent upon these people, who can bring tourists to them or decide to take tourists to another village. There are a few examples of hill tribe villages establishing modest tourism facilities on their own, but even in these cases the villagers remain dependent upon guide services to bring tourists to them. Those villages that have become the most dependent are likely to have also become more willing to give up their privacy and compromise some of their cultural values.

Tourism that is focused on expressions of ethnicity provides interesting examples of how different indicators and symbols of ethnic status can be negotiated. In the northern city of Chiang Mai, the local market does a sizable business in selling tribal handicrafts. Many of the least expensive of these goods are machine manufactured in Bangkok by ethnic Thai workers. The hawkers peddling the goods in Chiang Mai's market are often dressed in ethnic garb, although they do not always belong to the tribes whose "costumes" they have borrowed. This cultural borrowing for the purposes of tourism exists in other ways as well. A colleague who has worked in Thailand for a number of years once told me of his visit to a fairly remote tribal community. While he was there, several of the village leaders engaged him in a discussion of how they might attract more tourists to the area. The villagers felt that they had nothing special to attract attention to themselves—no interesting festivals, elaborate and distinctive clothing, or unique arts and crafts. One villager then suggested that a neighboring village performed good music and that they might "borrow" the music to perform for visitors.

In many countries, ethnic minorities are vulnerable to the negative effects of tourism because they have lost much of their control over their own affairs. There are other examples in which tourism has actually helped minority communities gain greater autonomy and independence, either as a result of income derived from tourism or as a result of their increased commodity value as part of a national or regional plan for tourism development. The initial, negative impacts of ethnic and nature tourism in the Indian state of Ladakh (including environmental degradation, profit leakage, and increased social tension) led to the founding of several local organizations, sponsored by student, community, and religious groups. The goal of these groups was to increase local tourism profits and to encourage a sustainable style of tourism that would do less harm to the region's cultural and environmental properties. One of these organizations convinced some tourists to give up part of their vacation in order to work with local people on campaigns to clean up the environment. Another organization has used fees collected from tourists to repair community temples. One student organization conducted tours for visitors and used the income from these tours to help pay the educational costs of minority students.

These potential benefits of ethnic tourism are not limited to cases in which minority populations so clearly suffer from exclusion. The Amish of Pennsylvania's Lancaster County provide an interesting example in this regard. Over the past several decades, the Amish successfully have resisted the alienation of their farmlands and the erosion of many of their distinct social conventions, precisely because they are so valuable to the region's economy as tourist attractions. They have become worth more as Amish than their lands might be worth if put to other uses.

In their study of tourism among Indonesian cultural minorities, Jean-Luc Maurer and Arlette Zeigler (1988) note that ethnic groups vary considerably in their abilities to accommodate tourism without experiencing radical cultural change. They also offer an accounting of what they feel are the important attributes for an ethnic group to have in order to accommodate tourism effectively. These are: (1) a high "degree of internal cohesion," which will help the group resist those elements of change that they perceive to be negative; (2) a "capacity for renewal," which will allow groups to assimilate some outside influences without harm to their overall cultural well-being; (3) an ability to "differentiate the sacred and the profane," permitting them to determine what aspects of their culture they can afford to commercialize and what aspects should be withheld from the market; and (4) sufficient "social solidarity" to "divide equally the economic benefits and social costs of intercultural contact."

In describing the successful adaptation to tourism on the part of the Sani, a Chinese ethnic minority, Margaret Bryne Swain (1990) notes that the Sani have been careful to avoid becoming overly dependent upon visitors to their region. Their economic development strategies include diversifying in other areas as well, such as goat farming. Swain suggests that economic dependence upon tourism would be dangerous for the Sani, because the Chinese government retains control over the amount of access tourists have to their villages.

As is apparent with the earlier mentioned example of the Amish in Pennsylvania, ethnic tourism does not always involve situations in which there are considerable social or economic differences between tourists and their "hosts." The United States is, for example, a nation of immigrants, many of whom seek opportunities to visit the countries from which their ancestors originated. Some host countries, which have experienced considerable out-migration during periods of their history, have come to base much of their tourism on inviting such people to return to their ethnic "roots." Ireland is a good example of this. In other cases, such as return visits to various Caribbean nations by U.S. residents of Caribbean ancestry, it is difficult to determine the line between being a tourist and belonging to a place. Although the conditions are quite different, several African nations have begun to offer tourist experiences that encourage African Americans and other blacks to discover their African heritage. The cultural implications of these kinds of ethnic tourism have been little studied and are not well understood.

In some cases, ethnic tourism might also involve opportunities to visit places that represent historical relationships between ethnic groups. Many tourist sites and shrines in the western United States focus on early relationships among Hispanic, Native American, and Anglo ethnic groups. Of late, there has been increased interest in tourism places that serve to represent slavery in the United States. Plantation sites that once focused almost exclusively on interpreting the lives and experiences of white landowners have begun to provide new interpretations of the living conditions of black slaves. Such sites are, of course, highly contestable in their interpretations.

A study of efforts to interpret the black experience at Virginia's Colonial Williamsburg (Gable, Handler, and Lawson 1992) notes that there has recently been an attempt to be more inclusive and "multicultural" in the presentation of such sites. The authors conclude, however, that there remains a disparity between how white and black histories are often interpreted. At Colonial Williamsburg, presentations of white history (focusing on the nation's "founding fathers") tend to be offered as factual and uncontestable. On the other hand, the presentations of black history are more conjectural and relativistic, and in this light their "truth" is perhaps less convincing. The authors of this study note that the interpreters of Colonial Williamsburg's black experience justify the conjectural nature of their presentations on a lack of knowledge about black history. The authors point out, however, that several decades of recent scholarship have provided considerably more historical knowledge of black history than is utilized at the site. They also question the way Colonial Williamsburg's curators represent the material cultures of both whites and blacks. In these cases, the attribution of a particular item of material culture is made on the basis of *ownership*, and since few blacks owned much at the time, their material culture is represented as sparse and limited to a few utilitarian items. The authors point out that attributions of material culture based on *use,* rather than ownership, would provide the means for a different interpretation. Black slaves regularly used the property of their owners, if only in service to them. The many objects that they used are as much a part of their material culture as it is of the culture of the white colonists.

THE LANGUAGE OF TOURISM

The example of Colonial Williamsburg underscores the importance of language in interpreting tourist places. Here, a language of fact and another of conjecture are used to describe two different histories. As the study's authors note, there is yet another discourse associated with the interpreters' descriptions of black history, and that is the language of "multiculturalism." Normally, it is facts that interest us as tourists. We do not have much reason to become interested in people or places about which little is known. In the case of Colonial Williamsburg's black history, however, the presumed lack of knowledge need not deter us, because current public discourse concerning black history directs us to the realization that this is something in which we all *should* be interested.

Language and discourse informs and helps shape tourism in several ways. They establish the means and patterns of communication between the various actors of tourism activities. Language is important in the marketing of tourism and in the interpretation of tourist experiences. It can also play a role in how local communities negotiate tourism opportunities within larger regional and national spheres of influence and domination.

Eric Cohen and Robert Cooper (1986) have noted that tourist languages are usually dominant in touristic exchanges. In most other cases of international exchange, people who come to another country (as guest workers or immigrants, for example) are expected to learn to communicate in the host language. Tourists are rarely expected to do so. Accordingly, much of the effort devoted to preparing workers for employment in the tourist industry is devoted to language training. By the same token, many of the frustrations and humorous occasions of international tourism result from language miscommunication.

While the language of the tourist tends to dominate touristic exchanges, certain "tourist languages" also dominate over other visitor languages. In many parts of the world, English is the major language of international exchange (in other places, it might be French or Spanish or Japanese). Tourists visiting these places from non-English-speaking nations often find themselves in the somewhat awkward position of having to communicate with the locals in a language that is foreign to them as well as to their hosts. In countries that rely heavily upon international tourism, tourism workers might specialize in particular foreign languages. In Thailand, for example, service workers (guides, waiters, prostitutes) might specialize in English, in a particular European language, or in Japanese.

An area that is ripe for linguistic research revolves around trying to determine the cultural implications of the ways in which international tourists and hosts exchange their languages. What, for example, are the modern touristic equivalents of the creolized and pidgin languages that are usually associated with earlier periods of trade and colonialism? Words convey ideas and concepts, and their analysis in touristic exchanges could help us sort out some of the social and cultural consequences of tourism. To my knowledge, very little work has been done in these areas.

On the other hand, considerably more research has been devoted to the uses of language in promoting and marketing tourism places and to defining the tourism experience once visitors arrive at their destinations. A survey of tourist brochures from different parts of the world will readily demonstrate how pervasive and standardized some of the images of tourism have become. Can there really be so many idyllic places with pristine natural settings, invariably smiling locals, delicious cuisines, and secure, comfortable tourist facilities? Tourist brochures appeal to our desires and in some respects help create new desires, often in quite subtle ways. The promotion of sex and sexual opportunity is, for example, commonplace. I cannot count the number of brochures I have seen that depict a young Thai woman gesturing with a *wei* (hands clasped before her face, head slightly bowed) in front of a much taller white male tourist. Brochures and advertisements for Caribbean places rarely fail to provide at least one picture of a bikini-clad woman frolicking in the sea. Some brochures for Amsterdam employ photographs and language that serve in unambiguous terms to advertise the city's popularity as a destination of gay and lesbian tourists.

Graham Dann (1996) has described some of the ways in which language is used to promote various kinds of tourism, as well as to regulate and control interactions between tourists and hosts. He indicates, for example, that language often plays a significant role in the socialization of tourists. The process he describes is one in which tourists are invited to play the role of a child about to explore new physical and cultural terrain. Their socialization begins with guidebooks and marketing brochures, which assure the tourist-child that his or her safety and comfort needs will be assured and that there will be plenty of opportunities to satisfy his or her biological and emotional needs. Once they have arrived at their destination, industry workers guide the tourist-child to a bed, even turning down the sheets, provide food, and offer the assurance of 24-hour contact with the front desk. Dann describes the work of other scholars who have suggested that this child-parent relationship persists throughout the traveler's visit. The goal of tourism industry representatives is to transform the tourist from the "natural Child (with unlimited wants) to the adapted Child (with trained needs)." This evolving relationship is expressed and reinforced through patterns of language use that encourage tourists to take advantage of the opportunity to be childlike, as well as to respect the higher authority and greater wisdom of hospitality management. One of the most interesting aspects of Dann's discussion concerns what happens when this communication breaks down. Tourists might, for example, react strongly to even minor signs that they are not being taken care of in proper fashion. A missing reservation or insufficient towels in a hotel can erupt into a childlike tantrum, especially if the "host" fails to maintain his or her parent role.

This is an intriguing explanation for some kinds of tourist behavior. It seems a far better interpretation than the more popular notion that so many tourists are just bad, inconsiderate people. I recall a conversation I once had with the owner of a small hotel in New Jersey. The way he discussed the trials and tribulations of his business was similar to the kinds of concerns that are often expressed by parents. You have to be on your toes all the time, day and night, because you can never really anticipate what your guests are going to do or what they might find to complain about. When guests do complain, you have to keep a cool head and suppress your own feelings. Still, there were good parts of the business too. This hotel owner had many clients who returned year after year, and who, he suggested, had become almost like family.

In his book, Dann also discusses several *registers* that are associated with the language of tourism. A register is a particular way of speaking that is associated with such factors as the status of the speaker, the communication medium, and what is being discussed. Dann provides the example of a lawyer, who participates in one kind of register when he appears in court and (hopefully) in an entirely different register when he is interacting with his children. Some of the registers that Dann associates with tourism are: (1) the *nostalgia* register; (2) *spasprech*, which is the register of health tourism; (3) *gastrolingo*, the register of food and drink; and (4) *greenspeak*, which is the register of ecotourism. Each of these registers, Dann asserts, can be linked to distinct conventions of language use and patterns of discourse.

Since we have touched less on the matter of food and drink in this book than we have on the three other registers mentioned, it might be appropriate now to explore that example. The terms of gastrolingo are often reflected in elite travel and food and drink magazines and conveyed to would-be tourists in travel brochures that extol the foods of particular regions and famed dining places. Like other aspects of tourism, food can be associated with issues of authenticity, such as claims for a region's "authentic chili" or a restaurant's "genuine bouillabaisse." Another feature of gastrolingo is the use of foreign words, especially French and Italian words, to describe dishes and ingredients. The language of food and dining also includes features of the nostalgic. For example, a city's restaurants might be represented as exemplars of the past, both in terms of the offering of particular cuisines and in respect to their identities as historic places. "Little Italies," "Chinatowns," and similar ethnic neighborhoods often derive much of their appeal for tourists on the basis of their food. A final characteristic of gastrolingo is its occasional association with guilt, inviting guests to indulge themselves, neglect calorie counting, and perhaps to "sin" a little in their gluttony. The vacation, as a respite from the disciplines of everyday life, seems to reinforce this discourse of indulgence. The megabuffets that are so popular at some tourist resort areas epitomize it. Dann does not fail to note the relatedness of overindulgence to his earlier discussion of the tourist as a child.

The associations of food with tourism are represented in other ways as well. For example, regional foods are often favored as souvenir gifts to be given to friends and family at the end of a trip. For many travelers, both domestic and international, the act of travel itself provides opportunities to sample different foods, ranging from the fare offered on foreign airlines to the local snacks offered by vendors at bus and train stops. I remember a trip on a narrow-gauge railroad that cut through the mountains of Costa Rica from Limón to the capital of San José. The train stopped at dozens of towns along the way, and vendors boarded at almost every stop to pedal locally produced food. The food at each stop was different, and experienced domestic travelers knew what to expect at each stop and waited patiently for the place that would provide their special treat. With the advent of automobile tourism, food has taken on added significance, ranging from fast-food chain restaurants to roadside produce stands that offer tourists the opportunity to obtain "fresh-from-the-fields" fruits and vegetables.

Although the language of tourism, whether it is about food or some other register, is bound to vary across cultures, it is difficult to ascertain the extent of this variation, simply because there are so few comparable studies outside the contexts of Western tourism. One interesting exception is Brian Moeran's (1983) account of the language of Japanese tourism. Moeran notes that the high value placed on international leisure travel is a relatively recent phenomenon in Japan. Although he concludes that many of the Japanese ways of speaking about travel and tourism seem to have been derived from Western travel experiences, there are some interesting exceptions. Until quite recently, for example, most Japanese travelers participated minimally in those aspects of "gastrolingo" that focused on regional and exotic foods (which, in the case of the Japanese, might be American and European cuisines). Even during the late 1960s, Moeran reports, many Japanese tourists brought with them as much of their own food as they could manage. Although more recent Japanese tourist brochures do encourage their readers to be more adventuresome in their sampling of cuisines, it is interesting to note the prevalence of Japanese restaurants in parts of the world that are frequented by Japanese businesspersons and leisure travelers.

Moeran also reports that Japanese tourists tend to associate places with status in particular ways. The Japanese regard the giving of travel souvenirs upon return home as important enough to have its own terminology (*omiyage bunka*, translated roughly as "souvenir culture"). Japanese travel brochures describe overseas shopping opportunities in ways that emphasize Japanese values, with an emphasis upon the giving of gifts and the association of particular goods with their places. It is, for example, deemed considerably more prestigious to have bought a Pierre Cardin tie in Paris or a Gucci handbag in Rome than it would be to have bought either item in a department store in Tokyo or, for that matter, in Chicago. Moeran likens this trait to a strong interest in "cultural markers" on the part of the Japanese. It extends to the very specific and detailed ways in which tourist sights are described. More so than is typical of most Western travel advertisements, Japanese tourists are invited to visit places featured in popular Western films, cafes frequently by famous artists, and a library room in Geneva that was used by Jean-Jacques Rousseau. All these details respond, according to Moeran, to a heightened "cultural consciousness" on the part of Japanese tourists. He also suggests that many of the cultural markers are directed toward female travelers. We have already noted the extent to which the Japanese tourist industry relied heavily in its beginning stages on encouraging women to set the precedence for leisure travel. Noting that many Japanese marriage arrangements still rely upon parents to help select suitable marriage partners for their children, Moeran informs us that, along with the more traditional skills expected of a good wife, many Japanese now feel that it is desirable for a young woman to have traveled abroad at least once before marriage. Most desirable, it would seem, is travel to Europe, which is the most prestigious destination for many Japanese. In Japanese travel brochures, the standards set by European destinations often make their way into descriptions of other places. Moeran notes how Japanese travel advertisements praise San Francisco for its "Mediterranean mood," compare Southeast Asian beaches to the south of France, and depict Macau as the "Monte Carlo of the East."

Most current research related to language and tourism has focused on ways in which the tourism industry has used particular language styles and conventions to attract tourists and then to try to manage their behavior. From a completely different direction, Tim Oakes (1998) has described how local communities might use and to some extent subvert the dominating language of tourism to serve their own ends. Oakes's study of tourism in modern China focuses on the country's efforts to encourage ethnic tourism, both to attract international tourists and as a means to better incorporate China's many ethnic minorities into nationalist ideology by emphasizing the continuities between their particular histories and Chinese national heritage and tradition. This effort, Oakes maintains, has become particularly important as Chinese leaders face the divisive and discontinuous impacts of rapid modernization.

Among the more interesting parts of Oakes's study are his descriptions of how some ethnic villages have used and manipulated the nationalist rhetoric of ethnic tourism to position themselves within the mainstream of China's heritage development. One Hmong village, for example, argued that it should have greater autonomy from regional tourism officials in directing tourism in its community because it was the "most representative" (*zui you daibiaode*) and the "most typical" (*zui you dianxingde*) of the Hmong villages. The villagers argued that these qualities, borrowed directly from the state's priorities for identifying communities that should be targeted for tourism, made them especially valuable to the government. In other cases described by Oakes, villages competed less with the tourism authorities and more among themselves for designations of authenticity that might position them to participate in state tourism initiatives. Again, they proved themselves to be adept at using the state language of tourism and heritage to make their cases. Oakes maintains that these and other instances show that the villagers are full if not equal partners in modern tourism. They are keenly aware of the "subjectivities" that determine such qualities as heritage representativeness, and sometimes they are also successful in manipulating these rhetorics to their particular advantage.

The local uses of the dominant languages of tourism are certainly not limited to China. In Maryland, where I now live, the state recently announced a competitive program to provide funding to help regions of the state develop heritage tourism programs. Around the state, local committees met to go over the state's request for proposals, in part to find out just what it was that the state meant by "heritage." Having made that determination, each region that decided to submit a proposal was faced with the task of describing how its particular communities' heritage could best be represented in relation to the state's priorities.

MATERIAL CULTURE, PERFORMANCE, AND THE BUILT ENVIRONMENT

Some aspects of a culture are visible to any observer. They are the material and performance expressions of a people. These might include the performance of music, dance, and festivals, and the making of distinctive styles of dress and other material objects. Also included is the built environment, such as the style in which houses and other buildings are made, or even the way entire communities and cities are planned and constructed, as well as the ways in which landscapes are modified through human intervention. Anthropologists usually conclude that these visible expressions of a society are closely tied to other, less-visible cultural traits, such as family and community structure and a people's worldview or the way they integrate their experience of the world into a system of meaning. Performances and material objects might be closely linked to a people's economic life. For example, many contemporary festivals find their origins in human efforts to mark changes in the agricultural cycle. In rural communities this function can still be very important. Objects of material culture might not only serve utilitarian functions but also important social and cultural functions. In many highland communities around the world, for example, distinctive clothing styles have served to express family alliances, ethnic differences, village origins, as well as marital and social status.

Material culture and performance provide the means to visualize another society. They can also afford tourists the opportunity to "possess" some part of another society, by purchasing handicrafts to take home or by photographing performances and places of particular interest. In these cases, tourism can sometimes alter the cultural functions of a material object or performance. Utilitarian objects, such as a basket or pot, might be reinterpreted as "art" or at least as "quaint" by tourists. Tourist interest in purchasing such objects might shift the local value of such an object from its domestic context to a market context. This shift can involve alterations in manufacturing techniques or in the kinds of materials used to craft the object or even changes in who makes the object. As this occurs, the tourist is no longer purchasing an object that represents particular domestic traditions of a country or of a people but is instead buying an artifact of the culture and traditions of tourism.

Whether or not the transition from other purposes to tourist objects and performances is bad or good for the producing community depends on many factors, some of which will be discussed in this section. What this transition means to the tourist and to scholars of tourism is another matter. We tend to trivialize tourist objects, and when their touristic nature becomes obvious, we are tempted to regard them as fakes. It is worth keeping in mind that, when a "host" community becomes dependent upon tourism to one extent or another, the goods that it produces specifically for tourists are as authentic in their own right as are any other objects.

Because the most visible (or, in the case of music, the most pleasantly audible) aspects of culture are an important part of tourist traditions, countries and regions that are interested in promoting tourism often encourage both the retention and diffusion of these cultural traits. In hotels and restaurants in Thailand, for example, visitors might be greeted by hostesses dressed in "traditional" fashion, even though it is unlikely hostesses were ever allowed to dress themselves in such an elaborate way during the periods in which this garb was fashionable. Elsewhere, minority peoples might be encouraged to continue wearing traditional clothing in order to appear more authentic to tourists. In the north of Thailand, it is becoming increasingly the case that travelers are more likely to see hill tribe people in traditional dress in villages that receive many tourists than they will find in more remote villages.

There is no question that the interests of tourists often serve to alter material and performance culture. The challenge is to figure out what, in specific cases, this means for the owners of such traditions. As noted earlier, we have a tendency to think of traditions as those behaviors and things that have remained unchanged for a long period of time. In reality, many traditions are highly adaptable to change, and, as we also noted before, they are invariably subject to reinterpretation in the present. A good example of this adaptability is American jazz. Few would argue that jazz is not a firmly established tradition within American society. But from its very beginning, the expression of jazz was dependent upon innovation and improvisation. While a few characteristics of jazz remain constant and serve to define the music, a basic idea of jazz is that no performance, even by the same performer, will ever be an exact rendition of another performance. Many other people regard their traditions and the objects that represent them in much the same way as we accept jazz as an ever changing tradition. The idea that traditions should remain constant and resistant to change is perhaps little more than the wistful longing of those who perceive themselves to have lost their own connections to the past.

The value and authenticity of any object of material culture or performance is probably best judged by its social vitality, rather than by how long it has been around. Some Indian communities of the northwest coast of Canada have managed to preserve much of the social context of their material culture by making a clear distinction between objects that they produce for their own ceremonial uses and similar objects that they make to sell to tourists. In other cases, tourist interest has helped revive traditional arts and crafts and perhaps even improved the "quality" of their production. This is true, for example, of many of the objects of material culture, such as jewelry and pottery, produced by Indians of the southwestern United States. Two factors seem to have contributed to the revival and elaboration of native arts in this region. The first was a strong interest on the part of non-Indian collectors in acquiring high-quality handwork for both aesthetic and investment reasons. The second was the ability of Indian people to control much of the market and to distinguish their productions from inferior "tourist" goods. This control has not only encouraged the continuation of traditional craft techniques but also the innovation of new designs and art objects within these traditional parameters.

Some scholars have suggested that the creation of cheap souvenirs for tourists leads to a decline in the quality of local arts and crafts. The examples offered above indicate that this is not necessarily so. For example, many inexpensive and poorly made tourist souvenirs can be found in the southwestern United States. They include such items as miniature totem poles, which have no association with southwestern Indian culture, and other "primitive-like" tokens that have been manufactured in other countries and only seem vaguely "Indian." The availability of such items seems to have had no impact on either the availability or the quality of other, distinctly local arts and crafts.

The production of arts and crafts and other objects of material culture for tourist consumption is often associated with a country's ethnic minorities and rural population. This is partly because these people are presumed to have maintained a more "traditional" way of life. It is also because, in many instances, their labor is cheap. The question arises, then, as to how much the producers actually profit from their manufactures. There seems to be considerable variation in this regard. As a rule, where producers have direct access to the marketplace, and can therefore negotiate prices directly with tourists, the profit seems to be reasonable. On the other hand, where the producers have to rely on intermediaries to bring their goods to market, the producers are often exploited. Annemarie Seiler-Baldinger (1988) reports that producers of tourist crafts from one Colombian village received "miserable prices" for the goods, but that the intermediaries who brought the goods to the tourist markets realized of profits of 700 to 1,500 percent.

In some cases, tourism might actually give rise to new craft industries that become firmly established in a community. This has become true, for example, of two industries in Mexico—the silver-crafting industry in Taxco and the distinctive pottery manufactures of the City of Tonalá. Such industries might over time give rise to folkloric accounts that serve to "authenticate" their origins. In Thailand, richly painted umbrellas and fans have become popular tourist souvenirs. Most of the umbrellas were hand painted in the village of Borsan, near Chiang Mai. The significance of Borsan's painted umbrellas has been conveyed in a story that is provided to tourists. This myth recounts how a young girl from the village of Borsan once saw a monk standing by the road. It was raining, and she was so disturbed by the poor and shabby condition of the monk's umbrella that she went home to get him another. Her own umbrella was, however, too plain to be a suitable gift for a monk, so she sat down and painted it with elaborate figures of flora and fauna. From this gesture, as the story goes, emerged the tradition of painted umbrellas. In reality, the umbrella "factory" at Borsan was begun in the 1950s, by a Chinese businessman from Chiang Mai.

Performance culture is also influenced by tourism. Some research suggests that the local meaning of festivals and dances can be lost when they become commodities to be performed for outsiders. In some cases, the demands of tourism encourage communities to perform their ceremonies out of sequence—during the tourist season, for example, rather than during the appropriate agricultural cycle. Similarly, the demands of tourism can encourage a community to perform particular ceremonies much more often than they would normally be performed, thereby causing them to lose some of their social and cultural power. In other cases, however, communities have managed to retain much of the local significance of their ceremonies, even when they are doubly used to entertain tourists. In Bali, where dancing performances serve both as important community events and as major tourist attractions, the performers often alter the performances they provide for tourists in subtle ways. The alterations make no difference in terms of the tourists' experiences, but they are obvious to community members, thereby protecting the local significance of the more original performances. Jill Sweet (1991) reports that some southwestern United States Indian communities appoint tribal police to watch tourists, preventing them from photographing or otherwise interfering in important ceremonies. Interestingly enough, Sweet suggests that most tourists actually appreciate these restrictions and regard them as an indication that the performances they are allowed to witness are more authentic because the communities have not sold out to tourism.

As we have observed in relation to other aspects of tourism, relationships regarding material culture and performance vary considerably from one situation to another. In some cases, tourism can provide new markets for arts and crafts and can help revive these traditions. In other cases, tourism can contribute to the alienation of particular objects and ceremonies from their social context, resulting in a loss to the "host" community. I suspect, however, that instances in which tourism is the major culprit in this regard are less common than a review of the scholarly literature might suggest. The availability of cheap, mass-produced clothing and housewares has contributed much more surely and pervasively to the demise of indigenous material culture.

TOURISM IN PLACE AND SPACE

Tourists visit places and, in doing so, they occupy spaces. For our purposes, the idea of *place* will be limited to its physicality. Places are specific, visually recognizable terrain—landscapes, ecosystems, monuments, villages, hotels and shopping malls. *Spaces*, on the other hand, represent the ways in which places are occupied, and they might be physical spaces, but they might also be more experiential spaces, such as emotional, fantasy, or sacred spaces. People and cultures vary considerably in the ways in which they relate to such spaces. For one type of Christian, a church can provide a space to listen to a sermon and occasionally participate in the singing of a hymn. For another kind of Christian, a church might provide a space for quiet contemplation, and for yet another kind it might be a space of active, spontaneous participation and testimony. Consider the spatial requirements necessary to provide particular individuals or groups a sense of privacy. For some people, nothing less than an eight-foot wall will do. For others, privacy is a state of mind that is only vaguely related to physical exclusion or barriers.

The construction and modification of places and spaces is a popular human activity, driven in many respects by considerations of economic gain and by the dynamics of political and social expression. Sharon Zukin (1991) has described some of these processes for our modern time as the creation of "landscapes of power." Tourism has become one of several players in what she describes as the dominant ideology of a market-driven culture. In this culture, landscapes become separated from their places and transformed into spaces that serve such purposes as to decontextualize the future (Disney World) or to decontextualize the past (Baltimore's Inner Harbor). The spaces of market culture are occupied by universal landscapes of consumption and consumerism, designed to compete with local moral landscapes that serve as more contextualized and particularistic expressions of citizenship. As applied to tourism development, Zukin would argue that many of the values associated with travel are being displaced by a market culture that measures its success solely in terms how much tourists are willing to spend. If such things as ethnicity or nature are of any value at all in this equation, that value is simply an expression of their market worth. While earlier critiques of capitalist economic systems focused on the social and political dynamics of particular modes of *production*, Zukin has argued that the market economy is now being driven more by transformations in the modes of *consumption*. She does not, however, argue that this process is complete or irreversible. Localities do resist these landscapes of power, and "men and women still want to live in specific places." People, whether they be visitors to a place or residents of that place, do still manage to find spaces of their own.

The politics of space and tourism are represented in numerous ways. Stephen Jett (1995) has recounted conflicts that have arisen between tourist and Native American uses of particular features of the southwestern United States landscape. For the Navajo, many of these features represent sacred spaces that need to be protected. Jett notes that the idea of restricting access to particularly sacred sites was practiced by the Navajo long before tourists became a significant factor. Even Navajo were not allowed access to some of their especially powerfully sacred places without having first gained adequate spiritual knowledge. The conflict arises when tourists seek access to such sites. Other conflicts have developed in association with the interpretation of sacred spaces. While specific knowledge pertaining to the Navajo's sacred use of the landscape might, on the one hand, encourage greater respect for these places on the part of visitors, Navajo leaders have cautioned that much of this knowledge is held in secret and that sharing such knowledge with outsiders could compromise the spiritual value of particular sites.

In other instances, conflicting uses and interpretations of spaces might be further complicated in that the "ownership" of these space's places has been contested for some time. An account concerning the Carnarvon Gorge National Park in Australia (Huggins, Huggins, and Jacobs 1995) is particularly poignant in this regard, in that two of the authors are Aboriginals, and the Carnarvon Gorge is in the process of being reclaimed by the Aboriginal people in a legal process. The authors recount with irony the difficulty that is inherent in having to "remember" for the courts the ways in which their people once occupied this space, particularly after having been encouraged for such a long time to forget any such associations.

Although Zukin's account of the role played by tourism in a new culture of consumption is persuasive in many respects, it should be noted that many places continue to derive their appeal to tourists because of their specific nature. These places serve as powerful symbols of locality that seem immune to any attempt to alienate them from their contexts. John Gold and Margaret Gold (1995) describe Scotland as one such place. For more than 200 years, tourism to Scotland has both reflected and in some respects helped shape the cultural and natural uniqueness of the country. Tourism has become a major way in which Scotland presents itself to the rest of the world. This presentation emphasizes highly sentimental and romanticized images of Celtic and Highland culture. The authors note that such a high degree of particularity has made it difficult for the country's tourism promoters to expand upon their successes by encouraging future tourists to visit Scotland to witness and participate in more modern representations of the country.

Our discussion of this topic has so far focused on differences between tourist and "host" expectations regarding the uses of places and spaces. We can also anticipate that there is significant cultural variation in the ways in which different tourists occupy places and spaces. Let us again take Japanese tourism as an example. It is interesting to note, for example, that there are differences in the ways Japanese and Westerners typically regard leisure spaces. John Horne (1998) has suggested that there is a fair measure of bias in Western observers' tendencies to stereotype the Japanese work ethic as allowing little space for leisure activities. He argues that the Japanese simply allocate leisure spaces differently. At least until quite recently, Japanese males tended to allocate little leisure time to be spent with their families. The division between work and leisure is not nearly so sharp in Japan as it is considered to be the West, with the result being that leisure is much more likely to occur in spaces shared by workmates. To the extent that this remains true, it points again to our relative neglect of business travel as a form of tourism. Japanese business travel is likely to include significant moments of leisure and recreational activity shared by colleagues, and these might indeed be very important and culturally determined expressions of tourism.

Nelson Graburn (1995) has pointed out that the Japanese have what may be the world's oldest tradition of domestic mass tourism. Contemporary domestic travel in Japan appears to reflect these earlier traditions in some cases and to depart from them in others. Reminiscent of earlier modes of tourism to famous shrines, Graburn notes the extent to which Japanese rural tourist sites remain dependent upon being associated with "famous things" (*meibutsu*). The famous things of Japanese rural tourism might include shrines, noted local products or produce, or natural phenomena such as famous volcanoes. While there are aspects of such behavior in Western rural tourism, it does seem that there is greater emphasis in the West upon experiencing rural places as being typical rather than particularly unique—this is a "good" tourist destination because it gives one a "real" sense of typical country life.

Graburn also notes that Japanese domestic tourism to rural places differs from similar experiences in the West in that many Japanese regard their excursions as opportunities to escape from the Westernized cities in which they reside. Whereas Western tourists might travel to their own rural places to explore continuities between the present and the past, Graburn's observation suggests that Japanese tourists experience a considerably greater disparity between their past and their present, which is perceived in many respects as being alien. Along with this, Graburn argues that modern Japanese have a "low sense of cultural self-confidence" compared to most Westerners. This means that they are more likely to seek rural tourist sites that are "culturally approved" and less likely to be attracted to travel opportunities that depart from traditional expectations. This tendency relates to other characteristics that Graburn attributes to Japanese rural tourism. He suggests, for example, that many Japanese remain suspicious and distrustful of nature. When they travel in nature, they are most likely to do so in groups and to stick to approved itineraries. They seem to like nature best when it is controlled, as it is in bonsai presentations and formal gardens.

I have to admit that I feel slightly uncomfortable with some of Graburn's remarks. They seem too stereotypical. In fairness to him, however, much of what he has to say has been reported by others. What Graburn refers to as a low sense of cultural self-confidence has been discussed by others as a consequence of the Japan's relatively rapid experience of modernization. Much of Brian Moeran's (1983) discussion of the language of Japanese tourism, mentioned above, makes similar points. John Knight (1993) also points to a number of Japanese rural tourism sites that promote themselves by making comparisons to European places and spaces. This practice is not, of course, limited to Japan. Tourist places in the United States, for example, do sometimes draw parallels to their associations with "Old World" places and sites. In this respect, it is perfectly reasonable to conclude that many Americans also retain a fair measure of lack of cultural self-confidence in respect to their ties with Europe.

We discussed in chapter 3 the extent to which the spaces of Japanese tourism might be gendered differently than they normally are in the West, partly as a result of the extent to which the Japanese tourism industry has encouraged young women to break new ground in tourism. This point was made by Marilyn Ivy (1995), who also has some interesting things to say about recent transitions in the development of Japanese domestic tourism. Ivy describes a Discover Japan campaign that was initiated in 1970 by the Japan National Railway. Focusing on young, urban women travelers, the campaign emphasized characteristics of travel that diverge from the traditions described by Graburn. The places depicted in travel advertisements had, for example, lost their specificity and their association with famous things, more closely approximating a generic appreciation of natural and rural places. The Discover Japan campaign was followed in 1984 by an Exotic Japan campaign, which encouraged travelers to explore places in Japan that represented non-Japanese (although not necessarily Western) culture. Many of these places stressed relationships with the non-Japanese Orient. Again, young women were frequently employed as icons of this new form of "exotic" domestic travel, although now the women were more likely to be featured as adventuresome, rootless, new-wave idols. According to Ivy, the Exotic Japan campaign soon shifted from a focus on foreign spaces within Japan to an imagery that presented Japan itself as a foreign country, encouraging the Japanese to view their own country with the eyes of foreigners. This campaign clearly recognized a fully urbanized "neo-Japanese" youth who were felt to have little connection with many of the objects and spaces that represented Japanese traditions and who instead associated broadly with the modern, Westernized spaces into which they had been born.

The analysis offered by Ivy describes a process of tourism modernization and postmodernization that is clearly related to Zukin's idea of the culture of consumption, although the patterns of consumption seem to be different for the Japanese to the extent that they have turned in on themselves to make exotic what would normally be thought to be familiar, at least by association if not by actual experience. Following Ivy's conclusions to an extreme, we might ask whether travel to the United States might for many young Japanese represent more of the characteristics of domestic travel (a return to one's roots, for example) than does travel within their own country.

What Ivy has described is a process related to the *globalization* of tourism, reflecting in this case the particularly complex relationships the Japanese have with the rest of the world. It remains for us to ask, in more general terms, whether such processes of globalization do indeed represent the future of modern tourism.

TOURISM IN GLOBAL AND LOCAL PERSPECTIVE

Anthropology first made its mark as a discipline that celebrated the local and sought to inform the world of its remarkable diversity. This enchantment with distant places did not last long and was perhaps always more an artifact of the ways in which the discipline was perceived by the general public than a reflection of its actual practices. Contemporary anthropologists remain interested in local places but are equally aware of the need to place specific localities within the larger contexts that are implied by such terms as *world systems*, *globalization*, and *transnationalism*. We have considered such issues throughout this book. Modern tourism is a consequence of both pervasive global forces and the particularity of specific places and peoples. In fact, tourism provides an excellent terrain for exploring the relationships between the global and the local.

As we noted in chapter 1, several theorists of tourism stress the homogenizing influences of tourism. These influences can encourage localities to attempt to refashion themselves into entities that conform to tourists' expectations. They also find much of their impetus in the tendency for all capitalistic enterprises, tourism included, to attempt to standardize their products, control their markets, and routinize patterns of consumption.

One fairly obvious influence in this regard is the increasing presence of transnational corporations and governmental entities that serve to direct the course of tourism development. Local, family-owned hotels and restaurants often lose out in competition with international hospitality corporations, lending a familiarity and predictability to travel that some tourists have come to expect and that others abhor. Similarly, as national governments ally themselves in regional trade agreements, they tend to focus more on what they have in common than on their differences and, as we have seen in regard to new political and economic entities such as the European Union, this has contributed to a tendency to "package" tourism along the lines of these common features.

Another impetus to the globalization of tourism is the increased economic dependency upon tourism that has been experienced in so many parts of the world, from major urban places to seemingly isolated villages. This dependency tends to leave tourists with a considerably greater range of choices than is often enjoyed by their "hosts." Tourist localities find it difficult to compete without regular infusions of new capital, and the price of their bargains with investors is often increased participation in the kinds of "postindustrial" market cultures described by Sharon Zukin in *Landscapes of Power* (1991).

Entrepreneurs like Thomas Cook and Fred Harvey were the precursors to a global travel industry. The business of this industry is twofold. One task is to try to tell potential tourists what they want and how to get it. The other is to produce places that conform to the expectations and desires the industry has helped create. To the extent that the travel industry succeeds in these aims, the resulting homogenization of the tourist experience seems obvious. So too, the experience of hosting, in which more people are likely to find the places they inhabit being transformed into sites for others to visit.

Another contributor to homogenization is international tourism training and education. The perceived need to provide tourists with predictable experiences has resulted in a profusion of schools and training centers devoted to preparing tourism workers and professionals to fulfill this need. Increasingly, this field has emphasized the desirability of training workers to global standards of hospitality (e.g., Go 1998). To the extent that this goal is realized, cultural and regional differences in maintaining hospitality norms are likely to be diminished, at least in regard to employment in major tourist facilities.

These forces of globalization within the tourist industry are readily apparent and difficult to dismiss. But are there countervailing tendencies that serve to modulate the drive for control and predictability? We have discussed several such tendencies in this book. To some extent, the tourism industry itself, along with competition within the industry, provides a degree of correction. Competition requires innovation. A market culture driven by consumption requires a steady supply of new products. The result, in respect to tourism, has been increased segmentation of the market, leading to emphases on newly stylized forms of travel, such as heritage tourism, ecotourism, adventure travel, and appropriate or alternative tourism. The industry has also become increasingly interested in adapting to the needs of particular kinds of tourists, such as older travelers, the handicapped, and gay and lesbian tourists. Admittedly, these travel concepts and "niches" can be altered in significant and often disappointing ways when they are transformed into global markets. On the other hand, their popularity indicates recognition on the part of the industry that the tastes and priorities of the traveling public are themselves shifting and that many tourists are seeking alternatives to the usual options offered by the industry.

Other trends in the tourism industry have also contributed to diversification. For example, the growing popularity of "bed-and-breakfast" accommodations has provided many tourists with alternatives to staying in chain hotels and motels. The increasing use of the Internet as a way for individuals to plan their holidays and travels has provided opportunities for small-scale, local tourism facilities to market themselves in ways that were previously unavailable.

There is considerable variation in the ways in which regions and communities respond to tourists in their midst. They do not always conform strictly to the expectations of visitors or to the demands of the tourism industry. In many cases, they adapt, resist, and even re-create the conditions of visitation. It is important to remember in this respect that anthropologists have tended to study tourism as it occurs in earlier, formative stages, usually among marginalized people. Less attention has been paid to those communities that have a longer-term experience with tourism, such as many of the Pueblo Indian communities in the southwestern United States. Here, and elsewhere, "hosts" have not only learned to accommodate tourism but have also endeavored to place limits and controls on the ways it affects their communities. In some instances, competition for tourists has resulted less in homogenization and more in a tendency for communities to differentiate themselves as unique destinations.

Anthropologists and other scholars of tourism sometimes fret over the extent to which contact with tourists can result in people abandoning their traditions and attempting to adopt the lifestyles of their visitors.

Scholars are not alone in having this concern. One of the most often-mentioned negative impacts of tourism, from the perspective of "host" communities, is the impact of tourist behaviors on local youth. Still, in several places in this book we have seen instances in which tourism serves to differentiate rather than homogenize human experience. The behaviors and lifestyles of tourists might encourage receiving communities to find new value in their own way of being. As we have noted, the idea that cultural distinctiveness is a result of isolation has influenced our view in this respect. There is equally compelling evidence that cultural contact through various experiences of translocality can lead to increased distinction in the forming of local identities (e.g., Abram and Waldren 1997). Another important aspect of this differentiation lies in recognizing that symbols of globalization might be used in quite different ways across cultures. The McDonald's down the street from me is a good example of certain American tastes and values, emphasizing speed of delivery over service and low cost over quality. It is the kind of place we do not always like to admit patronizing. The McDonald's that I visited in Bangkok looks the same, and the hamburgers seem even more bland. But the McDonald's in Bangkok is not valued for its food or for its fast service. It is a place where elite youth hang out to experiment with their cosmopolitan aspirations, a place to be seen rather than a source of social discomfort.

A final factor that serves to mitigate against the homogenization of tourism can be found in the desires and expectations of tourists of all kinds. As much as we are creatures of culture and subject to the social forces of our time, so do we also make choices and occasionally turn away from the mainstream. One of my first teachers of anthropology, Homer Barnett, advised his students that all social scientists were faced with a choice that would have an important influence on the way they went about their work. That choice was to decide whether humans are basically creative or whether they are mostly the victims of the social and cultural forces of their time. I have been grateful for this choice and have decided that, if my judgment must err, it should be on the side of human creativity. We hold within ourselves the fundamental mechanism that will defy all attempts to routinize our behaviors and unduly limit our desires.

EPILOGUE

I mentioned at the beginning of this book that I like to hang out in terminals. Sometimes I think they represent the future—a world in which the ways things are connected assumes as much importance as the things themselves. This morning I sit at my computer trying to finish a book. But my computer is a lot more than a place to store the words I am putting together. If I knew your e-mail address, I could send these thoughts to you right now. In a matter of minutes, I could be asking someone in South Africa what the weather is like there or be getting information I need to plan a trip to Ecuador. My computer, a kind of terminal in its own right, keeps me connected.

Actually, that is not quite accurate. It is my *software* that connects me. Easily portable, my software keeps me connected no matter where I happen to be. It connects me with my home when I am traveling and with other places when I am at home. For good and for bad, modern technology is closely associated with portability. The invention of the wristwatch helped make time our steadfast traveling companion. Portable radios and televisions have infiltrated the most remote places of the world. Camcorders and digital cameras serve to connect images to our traveling words. We have at our disposal a miscellany of portable appliances, ATM machines, mobile homes, cell phones, and computer notebooks.

Technology fuels and encourages our restlessness. The ideas of being at home and of being away take on new meanings when these two conditions become so entwined. My point is that travel is not simply an adjunct to civilization, dislocation is not an anomaly, and tourism is no longer a rare privilege. We are nearly all of us outfitted to go.

I have argued here for a view of tourism that admits to both the importance and the complexity of its subject matter. There is no easy way to generalize the consequences of tourism, although I have suggested that there are four factors that do seem to account for the diverse kinds of consequences that we are likely to observe. Attention to these can help us understand some of these differences.

The first factor is the tourist. We have seen that there are many ways to differentiate kinds of tourists and tourism. The consequences of tourism do not result solely from the presence of a certain number of visitors to a place but also from the specific activities in which these visitors are engaged. Most examples of tourism provided in this book focus on leisure-based tourism, but I have argued here for a broader definition that includes people who travel for other reasons. Broadly stated, tourism can be any activity that involves the self-conscious experience of another place. In chapter 1, we also noted that there has been a tendency to regard tourism as a fairly recent phenomenon, based on the traditions of elite Western travelers. I have challenged these assumptions by pointing to some studies that offer us glimpses into earlier nonelite and non-Western tourism traditions. Still, there are some characteristics that do seem specific to the development of modern tourism in the West. These include its association with the rise of industrial capitalism and the related emphasis on the recreational and transformational possibilities of travel.

Much of the scholarly literature devoted to tourism is concerned with issues of authenticity, and with evaluating the quality of the tourist experience. There is a clear difference of opinion as to whether tourists are people who delight in the crude superficiality of their experiences or are people who seek insightful encounters with genuine places and real people. I have suggested that they probably do both and that the differences between expressions of the "fake" and the "genuine" are not always as apparent as we might assume they are.

The second factor is that of the "host" community in which tourism occurs. Again, we have recognized that there is considerable variation in the ways in which local populations are linked to tourism, as well as in the kinds of communities that can become involved. We have identified a number of conditions that appear to be important in trying to understand the consequences of tourism in particular communities or regions. There is, for example, cultural variation in the ways people respond to visitors and to strangers. There can also be significant differences in the ways in which different segments of a community or region adjust to tourism— we have noted, for example, that youth sometimes respond more favorably and that women sometimes enjoy especially ambiguous relationships to tourism. There is evidence to suggest that communities involved with tourism fare better if their local economies are fairly diverse, keeping them from becoming overly dependent upon tourist dollars.

I believe the most important condition related to the adjustment of local populations that has been identified here is the degree of autonomy people have in deciding for themselves the terms by which they relate to tourism. This autonomy includes the ability to determine how and when tourists are admitted to a place, the ways in which particular parts of a culture can or should not be marketed and fashioned into commodities, and the determination of appropriate rules governing relationships between tourists and hosts.

The third factor is that of mediation, by which I refer to those persons and institutions that represent the tourism industry. These can include representatives of both the public and private sectors. We have noted that there is variation in the amount of control governments exert over the development of tourism and that interest in the development of tourism is expressed at many levels of authority, from the transnational to the local. I have also suggested that the "business" of tourism's mediators is not simply to accommodate tourists' desires but also to create new expectations and opportunities for travel. The motivation to mediate tourism generally has been assumed to be economic. Since tourism is one of the largest industries in the world, the wealth it generates is considerable. Still, I have argued here that tourism mediators are equally attracted to opportunities to use tourism to represent their cultural and ideological values. This adds another dimension to the complexity of our subject, since the cultural priorities associated with tourism development are rarely publicly stated or acknowledged.

The final factor is that of place. The consequences of tourism vary in relation to the places in which it occurs. We have seen, for example, that the social and economic impacts of tourism can be especially grave in places that are limited in area, such as beaches and small island communities. The scale of particular communities can influence the ways in which tourism is received. In a large city, there may be little difference between the activities of tourists and those of local residents. In a small village, on the other hand, the distinctions between resident and visitor behaviors can be glaring. The consequences of tourism can also be related to the prior uses of a place. For example, Baltimore's Inner Harbor development and Florida's Disney World, both discussed in this book, seem quite similar. Both are representative of what Sharon Zukin (1991) has called a new "culture of consumption." But the social impacts of the two developments have been quite different, in large part because Disney World was put in a place that few people were using, whereas the Inner Harbor was developed in the middle of city that was already experiencing considerable conflict concerning its future. Place does make a difference.

And tourism itself makes a difference. If I can hope for one overall impression to come out of this book, that is it. We are just beginning to realize how great a role tourism has come to play in shaping the way we understand and interpret our world. It has served to recreate many if not most of the places in which we live. It has helped redefine our relationships with other people. Modern tourism has profoundly altered the way we think about such things as travel and leisure. Collectively, the tourism industry is one of the largest employers in the world, so it also influences the manner in which many of us work. If it ever was so, tourism is no longer a trivial pursuit in any respect.

I hope you have found some things of interest in this book. If you cannot visit, do feel free to send a message (echambers@anth.umd.edu).

References

Abram, Simone, and Jacqueline Waldren, eds. 1997. *Tourists and Tourism: Identifying with People and Places*. New York: Berg.

Adams, Vicanne. 1992. "Tourism and Sherpas, Nepal: Reconstruction of Reciprocity." *Annals of Tourism Research* 19(4): 534–54.

Babcock, Barbara A. 1994. "Pueblo Cultural Bodies." *Journal of American Folklore* 107(423): 40–54.

Baldacchino, Godfrey. 1997. "Global Tourism and Informal Labor Relations: The Small-Scale Syndrome at Work." London: Mansell.

Bendix, Regina. 1989. "Tourism and Cultural Displays: Inventing Tradition for Whom?" *Journal of American Folklore* 102(404): 131–46.

Blundell, Valda. 1995. "Riding the Polar Bear Express; and Other Encounters Between Tourists and First Peoples in Canada." *Journal of Canadian Studies* 30(4): 28–51.

Bodley, John H. 1976. *Anthropology and Contemporary Human Problems*. Menlo Park, California: Cummings.

Boissevain, Jeremy, ed. 1996. *Coping with Tourists: European Reactions to Mass Tourism*. Providence, RI: Berghahn Books.

Bolles, A. Lynn. 1997. "Women as a Category of Analysis in Scholarship on Tourism: Jamaican Women and Tourism Employment." In *Tourism and Culture: An Applied Perspective*. Erve Chambers, ed. Albany: State University of New York Press.

Boo, Elizabeth. 1990. *Ecotourism: The Potential and Pitfalls. Vols. I & II*. Washington, DC: World Wildlife Fund.

Boorstin, Daniel J. 1961. *The Image: A Guide to Pseudo-Events in America*. New York: Harper & Row.

Boyd, W. E., and G. K. Ward. 1993. "Aboriginal Heritage and Visitor Management." In *Heritage Management in New Zealand and Australia*. C. Micahel Hall and Simon McArthur, eds. Oxford: Oxford University Press.

Brear, Holly Beachley. 1995. *Inherit the Alamo: Myth and Ritual at an America Shrine*. Austin: University of Texas Press.

Britton, Stephen, and William Clarke, eds. 1987. *Ambiguous Alternatives: Tourism in Small Developing Countries*. Suva, Fiji: University of South Pacific Press.

Bruner, Edward M. 1999. "Abraham Lincoln as Authentic Reproduction: A Critique of Postmodernism." *American Anthropologist* 96(2): 397–415.

Bruner, Edward M., and Barbara Kirshenblatt-Gimblett. 1995. "Maasai on the Lawn: Tourism Realism in East Africa." *Cultural Anthropology* 9(4): 435–70.

Bryman, Alan. 1995. *Disney and His Worlds*. London: Routledge.

Buck, Roy C., and Ted Alleman. 1979. "Tourist Enterprise Concentration and Old Order Amish Survival: Explorations in Productive Coexistence." *Journal of Travel Research* 18(1): 15–20.

Burke, Peter. 1995. "The Invention of Leisure in Early Modern Europe." *Past and Present* 46: 136–50.

Caslake, John. 1993. "Tourism, Culture and the Iban." In *Tourism in Borneo: Issues and Perspectives*. Victor T. King, ed. Wilmington, VA: Borneo Research Council.

Chambers, Erve, ed. 1997. *Tourism and Culture: An Applied Perspective*. Albany: State University of New York Press.

Clifford, James. 1997. *Routes: Travel and Translation in the Late Twentieth Century*. Cambridge, MA: Harvard University Press.

Cohen, Eric. 1982. "Thai Girls and Farong Men." *Annals of Tourism Research* 9(3): 403–28.

———. 1983. "Hill Tribe Tourism." In *Highlanders of Thailand*. J. McKinnon and W. Bhruksasru, eds. Kuala Lumpur: Oxford University Press.

———. 1996. "Hunter-gather Tourism in Thailand." In *Tourism and Indigenous Peoples*. Richard Butler and Thomas Hinch, eds. London: International Thompson Business Press.

Cohen, Eric, and Robert L. Cooper. 1986. "Language and Tourism." *Annals of Tourism Research* 13(4): 553–63.

Crick, Malcolm. 1989. "Representation of International Tourism in the Social Sciences." In *Annual Review of Anthropology* 18. Palo Alto, CA: Annual Reviews.

Dann, Graham M. S. 1996. *The Language of Tourism: A Sociolinguistic Perspective*. Oxon, England: Cab International.

De Kadt, Emanuel. 1979. *Tourism: Passport to Development?* London: Oxford University Press.

Dogan, Hasan Zafer. 1989. "Forms of Adjustment: Sociocultural Impacts of Tourism." *Annals of Tourism Research* 16(3): 237–53.

Duggan, Betty J. 1997. "Tourism, Cultural Authenticity, and the Native Crafts Cooperative: The Eastern Cherokee Experience." In *Tourism and Culture: An Applied Perspective*. Erve Chambers, ed. Albany: State University of New York Press.

Edington, John M., and M. Ann Edington. 1997. "Tropical Forest Ecotourism: Two Promising Projects in Belize." In *Tourism & Sustainability: Principles to Practice*. Michael Slabler, ed. Oxon: Cab International.

Evans-Pritchard, Deidre. 1989. "How 'They' See 'Us': Native American Images of Tourists." *Annals of Tourism Research* 16(1): 89–105.

Fjellman, Stephen M. 1992. *Vinyl Leaves: Walt Disney World and America*. Boulder, CO: Westview Press.

Forestell, Paul H. 1993. "If Leviathan Has a Face, Does Goia Have a Soul? Incorporating Environmental Education in Marine Eco-tourism Programs." *Ocean & Coastal Management* 20(2): 267–82.

Gable, Eric, Richard Handler, and Anna Lawson. 1992. "On the Uses of Relativism: Fact, Conjecture, and Black and White at Colonial Williamsburg." *American Ethnologist* 19(4): 791–805.

Go, Frank M. 1998. "Globalization and Emerging Tourism Education Issues." In *Global Tourism*. William F. Theobold, ed. Oxford: Butterworth-Heinemann.

Gold, John R., and Margaret M. Gold. 1995. *Imagining Scotland: Tradition, Representation and Promotion in Scottish Tourism since 1750*. Aldershot: Scolar Press.

Graburn, Nelson H. 1983. "The Anthropology of Tourism." *Annals of Tourism Research*. 10(1): 9–33.

———. 1995. "The Past in the Present in Japan: Nostalgia and Neo-Traditionalism in Contemporary Japanese Domestic Tourism." In *Change in Tourism: People, Places, Processes*. Richard Butler and Douglas Pearce, eds. New York: Routledge.

Graburn, Nelson H., and Roland S. Moore. 1994. "Anthropological Research on Tourism." In *Travel, Tourism, and Hospitality Research*. J. R. Brent Richies and C. R. Goeldner, eds. New York: John Wiley & Sons.

Greenwood, Dayvdd J. 1989. "Culture by the Pound: An Anthropological Perspective on Tourism as Cultural Commodization." In *Hosts and Guests: The Anthropology of Tourism*. Valene L. Smith, ed. Philadelphia: University of Pennsylvania Press.

Grimsley, Kristin Downey. 1999. "The World Comes to the American Workplace." *Washington Post* March 20: 1, 12.

Hall, Michael Colin, and Margaret E. Johnston. 1995. *Polar Tourism: Tourism in the Arctic and Antarctic Regions*. New York: John Wiley & Sons.

Hampton, Mark P. 1998. "Backpacker Tourism and Economic Development." *Annals of Tourism Research* 25(3): 639–60.

Handler, Richard, and Jocelyn Linnekin. 1984. "Tradition, Genuine or Spurious." *Journal of American Folklore* 97(2): 273–90.

Handler, Richard, and William Saxon. 1998. "Dyssimulation, Reflexivity, Narrative, and the Quest for Authenticity in 'Living History.'" *Cultural Anthropology* 3(3): 242–60.

Helms, Mary W. 1988. *Ulysses' Sail: An Ethnographic Odyssey of Power, Knowledge, and Geographical Distance*. Princeton, NJ: Princeton University Press.

Hitchcock, Robert K. 1997. "Cultural, Economic, and Environmental Impacts of Tourism among Kalahari Bushmen." In *Tourism and Culture: An Applied Perspective*. Erve Chambers, ed. New York: State University of New York Press.

Hobsbawn, Eric, and Terence Ranger, eds. 1983. *The Invention of Tradition*. Cambridge: Cambridge University Press.

Honey, Martha. 1999. *Ecotourism and Sustainable Development: Who Owns Paradise?* Washington, DC: Island Press.

Horne, John. 1998. "Understanding Leisure Time and Leisure Space in Contemporary Japanese Society." *Leisure Studies* 17: 37–52.

Horwich, R. H., and J. Lyon. 1993. *A Belizean Rain Forest: The Community Baboon Sanctuary*. Gay Mills, Wisconsin: Orang-utan Press.

Hsiung, David. 1997. *Two Worlds in the Tennessee Mountains: Exploring the Origins of Appalachian Stereotypes*. Lexington: University Press of Kentucky.

Huggins, Jackie, Rita Huggins, and Jane M. Jacobs. 1995. "Kooramindanjie: Place and the Postcolonial." *History Workshop Journal* 39: 165–81.

Hughes, George. 1995. "The Cultural Construction of Sustainable Tourism." *Tourism Management* 16(1): 49–59.

Hunter, Colin, and Howard Green. 1995. *Tourism and the Environment: A Sustainable Relationship*. New York: Routledge.

Ivy, Marilyn. 1995. *Discourses of the Vanishing: Modernity, Phantasm, Japan*. Chicago: University of Chicago Press.

Jett, Stephen C. 1995. "Navajo Sacred Places: Management and Interpretation of Mythic History." *Public Historian* 17(2): 39–47.

Kanga, Patrick, Mary Shave, and Paul Shave. 1995. "Economics of an Ecotourism Operation in Belize." *Environmental Management* 19(5): 669–73.

Keena, Margaret E. 1993. "Return Migrants and Tourism Development: An Example from the Cyclades." *Journal of Modern Greek Studies* 11(1): 75–95.

Knight, John. 1993. "Rural *Kukusaika*? Foreign Motifs and Village Revival in Japan." *Japan Forum* 5(2): 203–16.

Kohn, Tamara. 1997. "Island Involvement and the Evolving Tourist." In *Tourists and Tourism: Identifying with People and Places*. Simone Abram and Jacqueline Waldren, eds. New York: Berg.

Little, Cheryl. 1996. "Principles of Sustainability." *Environmental Action* 28(1&2): 9.

Lujan, Carol Chiago. 1993. "A Sociological View of Tourism in an American Indian Community: Maintaining Cultural Integrity at Taos Pueblo." *American Indian Culture and Research Journal* 17(3): 101–20.

Lundgren, Nancy. 1993. "Women, Work and 'Development' in Belize." *Dialectical Anthropology* 18(4): 363–78.

MacCannell, Dean. 1989. *The Tourist: A New Theory of the Leisure Class*. New York: Shocken.

Macdonald, Sharon. 1997. "A People's Story: Heritage, Identity and Authenticity." In *Touring Cultures: Transformations of Travel and Theory*. Chris Rojek and John Urry, eds. New York: Routledge.

Martinez, D. P. 1990. "Tourism and the *Ama*: The Search for a Real Japan." In *Unwrapping Japan: Society and Culture in Anthropological Perspective*. Eyal Ben-Ari, Brian Moerman, and James Valentine, eds. Honolulu: University of Hawaii Press.

Matthiesen, Peter. 1987. *The Snow Leopard*. New York: Penguin Books.

Maurer, Jean-Luc, and Arlette Zeigler. 1988. "Tourism and Indonesian Cultural Minorities." In *Tourism: Manufacturing the Exotic*. Pierre Rossel, ed. Copenhagen: International Work Group for Indigenous Affairs.

McClaurin, Irma. 1996. *Women of Belize: Gender and Change in Central America*. New Brunswick, NJ: Rutgers University Press.

McMinn, Stuart, and Eriet Carter. 1998. "Tourist Typology: Observations from Belize." *Annals of Tourism Research* 25(3): 675–99.

Mehta, Gita. 1979. *Karma Cola: Marketing the Mystic East*. New York: Ballantine Books.

Meisch, Lynn A. 1995. "Gringas and Otavalenos: Changing Tourist Relations." *Annals of Tourism Research* 22(2): 441–62.

Michaud, Jean. 1997. "A Portrait of Cultural Resistance: The Confinement of Tourism in a Hmong Village in Thailand." In *Tourism, Ethnicity, and the State in Asian and Pacific Societies*. M. Picard and R. E. Woods, eds. Honolulu: University of Hawaii Press.

Moeran, Brian. 1983. "The Language of Japanese Tourism." *Annals of Tourism Research* 10(1): 93–108.

Nash, Dennison. 1996. *Anthropology of Tourism*. Tarrytown, NY: Elsevier Science, Inc.

Noritake, Kanzaki. 1992. "The Travel-loving Tradition of the Japanese." *Japan Echo* 19(4): 66–9.

Nozawa, Hiroko. 1995. "Female Professionals in the Japanese Tourism Industry." *Annals of Tourism Research* 18(3): 484–87.

Oakes, Tim. 1998. *Tourism and Modernity in China*. New York: Routledge.

Picard, Michel, and Robert E. Wood, eds. 1997. *Tourism, Ethnicity, and the State in Asian and Pacific Societies*. Honolulu: University of Hawaii Press.

Pizam, Abraham, and Yoel Mansfeld, eds. 1996. *Tourism, Crime and International Security Issues*. New York: John Wiley & Sons.

Pratt, Mary Louise. 1992. *Imperial Eyes: Travel Writing and Transculturation*. New York: Routledge.

Pruitt, Deborah, and Suzanne LaFont. 1995. "For Love and Money: Romance Tourism in Jamaica." *Annals of Tourism Research* 22(2): 422–40.

Richter, Linda K. 1989. *The Politics of Tourism in Asia*. Honolulu: University of Hawaii Press.

Ritzer, George, and Allan Liska. 1997. "'McDisneyization' and 'Post-Tourism': Complementary Perspectives on Contemporary Tourism." In *Touring Cultures: Transformations of Travel and Theory*. Chris Rojek and John Urry, eds. New York: Routledge.

Rodriquez, Sylvia. 1998. "Fiesta Time and Plaza Space: Resistance and Accommodation in a Tourist Town." *Journal of American Folklore* 111(439): 39–56.

Seiler-Baldinger, Annemarie. 1988. "Tourism in the Upper Amazon and Its Effects on the Indigenous Population." In *Tourism: Manufacturing the Exotic*. Pierre Rosel, ed. Cophenhagen: International Work Group for Indigenous Affairs.

Shuji, Takashima. 1992. "Rambling Through the Edo Peiod." *Japan Echo* 19(4): 64–5.

Sieber, R. Timothy. 1997. "Urban Tourism in Revitalizing Downtowns: Conceptualizing Tourism in Bostom, Massachusetts." In *Tourism and Culture: An Applied Perspective*. Erve Chambers, ed. Albany: State University of New York Press.

Sindiga, Isaac. 1996. "International Tourism in Kenya and the Marginalization of the Waswahili." *Tourism Management* 17(6): 425–32.

Smith, Valene L. 1989. *Hosts and Guests: The Anthropology of Tourism*. Philadelphia: University of Pennsylvania Press.

———. 1996. "Indigenous Tourism: The Four Hs." In *Tourism and Indigenous Peoples*. Richard Butler and Thomas Hinch, eds. London: International Thomapson Business Press.

Swain, Margaret Byrne. 1990. "Commoditizing Ethnicity in Southwest China." *Cultural Survival Quarterly* 14(1):26–30.

Sweet, Jill D. 1991. "'Let 'em Loose': Pueblo Indian Management of Tourism." *American Indian Culture and Research Journal* 15(4): 59–74.

Towner, John. 1996. *An Historical Geography of Recreation and Tourism in the Western World 1540-1940*. New York: John Wiley & Sons.

Tucker, Josiah. [1757] N.d. *Instructions for Travelers*. New York: Johnson Reprint Corporation.

Turner, Victor. 1969. *The Ritual Process*. Chicago: Aldine.

Turner, Victor, and Edith Turner. 1978. *Image and Pilgrimage in Christian Culture*. New York: Columbia University Press.

Twain, Mark. [1897] 1989. *Following the Equator: A Journey Around the World*. New York: Dover Publications.

Urry, John. 1992. "The Tourist Gaze 'Revisited.'" *American Behavioral Scientist* 36(2): 172–86.

Waldren, Jacqueline. 1997. "We Are Not Tourists—We Live Here." In *Tourists and Tourism: Indentifying with People and Places*. Simone Abram and Jacqueline Waldren, eds. New York: Berg.

Ward, Martha C. 1993. *The Hidden Life of Tirol*. Prospect Heights, IL: Waveland Press.

Wearing, Stephen, and Libby Larsen. 1996. "Assessing and Managing the Sociocultural Impacts of Ecotourism: Revisiting the Santa Elena Rainforest Project." *The Environmentalist* 16: 117–33.

Weaver, David B. 1998. *Ecotourism in the Less Developed World*. New York: CAB International.

Weigle, Marta. 1992. "Exposition and Mediation: Mary Colter, Edna Fergusson, and the Santa Fe/Harvey Popularization of the Native Southwest, 1902–1940." *Frontiers* 13(3).

Weiner, Annette B. 1992. *Inalienable Possessions: The Paradox of Keeping-While-Giving*. Berkeley: University of California Press.

Wood, R. C. 1994. "Some Theoretical Perspectives on Hospitality." In *Tourism: The State of the Art*. A. V. Seaton, ed. New York: John Wiley & Sons.

Woods, Louis A., Joseph M. Perry, and Jeffery W. Steagall. 1994. "Tourism as a Development Tool: The Case of Belize." *Caribbean Geography* 5(1): 1–19.

Zerubavel, Yael. 1995. *Recovered Roots: Collectible Memory and the Making of Israeli National Tradition*. Chicago: University of Chicago Press.

Zukin, Sharon. 1991. *Landscapes of Power: From Detroit to Disney World*. Berkeley: University of California Press.

Index

Aboriginals (Australia), 87, 115
Adams, Vicanne, 41
Adaptation, settlement and, 4
Aesthetic harmony, 89
Africa
    environmental destruction in, 70
    host-guest similarities and, 103
    nature tourism in, 75
African Americans, 103, 104
Aggression strategy, 57
Akha villages, 101
Alamo, 50
Alarde festival, 95–96
Amish tourism, in Pennsylvania, 65–66, 102–3
Antarctic, 79
Anthropology, 120–21
Appalachia, 14, 16–17
Applied anthropology, 2
Art. See Material culture
Art colony, in New Mexico, 25
Asia. See also specific countries
    ethnic tourism in, 100
    touring, work, and leisure in, 8
Australia, 87
Authenticity of experience, 68, 97, 98–99, 122–23

Babcock, Barbara, 25–26
Baldacchino, Godfrey, 41, 42
Bali, 44–45, 113
Baltimore, Inner Harbor area, 51–53, 54
Bangkok, Thailand, 37
Basque identity, 95–96

Beach tourism, 72, 78
Bed-and-breakfast accommodations, 120
Belize, ecotourism in, 90–92
Bendix, Regina, 96
Blundell, Valda, 84
Boissevan, Jeremy, 56–57
Bolles, A. Lynn, 61
Boo, Elizabeth, 77
Boorstin, Daniel, 18–19, 21
Borneo, 67–68, 84
Borsan. See Chiang Mai (Thailand)
Boundaries, 48, 55
Boyd, W. E., 87
Brear, Holly Beachley, 50
Britton, Stephen, 70
Bruner, Edward, 76, 97
Bryman, Alan, 98
Built environment, 110–14
Burke, Peter, 7
Bushmen people, 70
Business, tourism as, 12–17

Canada, indigenous tourism in, 84
Capitalism, 13, 96–97
Caribbean region, 41, 79, 85, 103
Carnarvon Gorge National Park (Australia), 115
Carrying capacity, of tourist location, 35
Casino gambling, 39
Caslake, John, 84
Central America, Belize and, 90–92
Cherokee Indians, in North Carolina, 99
Chiang Mai (Thailand), 102, 113

Childlike state of tourist, 106–7

China, 103, 109

Citizens, home country responsibility for, 46

"Civilization." *See also* Culture(s); Indigenous peoples
    spread through tourism, 16–17 , 95

Civil Rights Museum (Memphis), 93–94

Clarke, William, 70

Classes, elites, masses, and, 8–11

Clifford, James, 3

Coastal zones, 77–78

Cohen, Eric, 82, 83, 101, 105

Colonial Williamsburg, black history and, 104

Colter, Mary, 25, 27

Commodification, 94

Communitas, tourist bonding and, 20

Communities, tourism and, 55–57, 86–90

Competition, in tourism, 120

Computers, connections via, 121–22

Cook, Thomas, 12–13, 17

Cooper, Robert, 105

Cooperation, international, 47–48

Costa Rica, 9, 74–75, 87

Covert resistance strategy, 56

Craft industries, 113. *See also* Ethnic tourism; Material culture

Crime, 59

Critical theory, 2

Cultural borrowing, for tourism, 102

Cultural markers, Japan and, 108–9

Culture(s). *See also* Appalachia
    beach tourism and, 78
    concept of, 2
    Hispanic, 17
    impact of tourism on, 120–21
    in locales of tourist origin, 10
    material, 110–14
Native American, 17
    nature tourism and, 76, 77
    people as nature and, 79–84
    as process, 3

Dann, Graham, 106–7

De Kadt, Emanuel, 36

Democracy, 89

Developing nations, 49

Discover Japan campaign, 117–18

Discrimination, 38

Disney theme parks, 29–30, 98

Displacement, 3–4

Diversification, 120

Dogan, Hasan Zafer, 55, 57

Dominica, 72, 85

Duggan, Betty, 99

Economic development, 32–39

Economy. *See also* Economic development; Political economy; Wealth
    travel and, 5

Ecotourism, 84–92

Edington, J. M., 91

Edington, M. A., 91

Edo period (Japan), 6–7

Educational experiences, 74

Elites
    and first-class tourists, 38
    masses and, 8–11

Embedded tourism, 73

Employment
    holidays, vacations, and, 17
    in tourism, 40–42
    of women in tourism, 61

English. *See also* Language of tourism
    as tourist language, 105

Environment
    built, 110–14
    ecotourism and, 84–90
    movement to "natural," 13–14
    nature, tourism, and, 67–92

Ethnic balance, tourism and, 54–55

Ethnic tourism, 100–104

Ethnography, 2

Europe
    reactions to mass tourism in, 56–57
    tourism initiatives in, 47

Europeans, travel by, 4–5

European Union, 47, 119

Evans-Pritchard, Dierdre, 26

Experience. *See* Authenticity of
    experience

Fencing strategy, 57
Fergusson, Erna, 25
First-class tourism, wealth and, 37–
    38
Fjellman, Stephen, 30
Food and drink, 107–8
Forestell, Paul, 86
Formosa. *See* Taiwan
"Forms of Adjustment" (Dogan), 55
Frontier experience, 74

Gazing, by tourists, 22
Gender, 59–63
Geopolitical boundaries, 48
Globalization of tourism, 118–21
Gold, John, 116
Gold, Margaret, 116
Golden Triangle, 48
Gorilla population, nature tourism
    and, 76
Governments, political behavior and,
    42–44
Graburn, Nelson H., 20, 21, 116–17
Grassroots tourism developments,
    53–54
Green, Howard, 69
Greenwood, Davydd, 95
Grimsley, Kirsten Downey, 59
Guests. *See* Host and guest

Habitats, indigenous tourism and,
    80
Hampton, Mark, 38
Handicrafts, indigenous tourism
    and, 81
Handler, Richard, 97
Harvey, Fred, 24–25, 27
"Harvey Girls," 25
Healing, indigenous tourism and,
    81–82
Helms, Mary, 5, 8
Heritage, indigenous tourism and,
    80–81
Hiding strategy, 56–57
Hill tribes, in Thailand, 100–102
Hispanic cultures, 17, 50

Historical issues and relationships
    ethnic tourism and, 103–4
    evidence about tourism, 4–12
    indigenous tourism and, 81
Hitchcock, Robert, 70
Hmong people, 100–101, 109
Hobsbawn, Eric, 97
Holidays, 17
Homogenization of tourism, 118–21
Horne, John, 116
Horwich, Robert, 90
Hospitality
    global standards of, 119–20
    industries in, 30
    industry of, 10–11
    role of, 11
    tourism and, 10
Host and guest, 30, 123
    boundaries between, 3
    problematic nature of "host" cat-
        egory, 58–59
    relationship between, 10
    social/economic similarities
        between, 103
Hotels, 13
Hsiung, David, 14, 17
Hughes, George, 89
Hunter, Colin, 69
Hunting, 71–72

Iban people, 84
India, 102
    nature tourism in, 76
Indigenous peoples, 79
    tourism interest in, 38–39
Indonesia, 44
    tourism among cultural minori-
        ties in, 103
Industrialization, tourism and, 13–
    14
Informal economy, 36–37
Inner Harbor (Baltimore), 51–53
Intellectual benefits, of travel, 16
Interlaken, Switzerland, 96
International agreements, 46
Interpretive anthropology, 2
Ireland, 103
Islands, 79
    beach tourism and, 78–79

Isle of Skye, 53–54
Israel, 50
Ivy, Marilyn, 61, 117–18

Jamaica, environment of, 70–71
Japan, 58
    female travel and, 60–61
    history of tourism in, 6–7
    language of tourism and, 108–9
    women in tourism and, 62
    work and leisure in, 116
Jett, Stephen, 115

Kalahari Desert region, 70
Kenna, Margaret, 59
Kenya, 86
    society of, 54–55
Kirshenblatt-Gimblett, Barbara, 76
Knowledge, travel and, 5
Kohn, Tamara, tourist typology of, 22
Kuna Indians, nature tourism and, 76

Ladakh, India, 102
Land resources. *See also* Environment
    in Jamaica, 71
Landscape. *See* Ecotourism; Environment
Language of tourism, 104–10
Larsen, Libby, 87
Latin America, 8. *See also* specific countries
Leakage. *See* Repatriation of profits (leakage)
Leisure, tourism and, 5, 7, 18
Lifestyles, tourist explorations of, 14
Liminality, 20
Linguistic research, language of tourism and, 105
Linnekin, Jocelyn, 97
Liska, Allan, 19, 21
Little, Cheryl, 88–89
Local populations, 23
Low-budget tourism, 38
Lujan, Carol Chiago, 26
Lundgren, Nancy, 92
Lyon, Jon, 90

Maasai people, 76, 81
MacCannell, Dean, 20, 21, 95, 97
Macdonald, Sharon, 53–54
Manipulation, in Disney World, 30
Marine life, 72
Market culture, 114–15
Market segmentation, in tourism industry, 84
Martinez, D. P., 58
Marxist interpretations, 96
Masada, 50
Masses, elites and, 8–11
Mass tourism, 9–10, 116
Material culture, performance, built environment, and, 110–14
Matthiessen, Peter, 73–74
Maurer, Jean-Luc, 103
Mayan people, 91
McCannell, Dean, 18
Meanings, reconciliation of, 23
Mediated activity, 30, 123
Mehta, Gita, 38
Mexico, 86
    craft industries in, 113
Middle class, tourism of, 10
Minority groups. *See* Ethnic tourism
Mlabri people, 82–83
Modern tourism, 12–17
Moeran, Brian, 108–9, 117
Moken people, 83
Monkeys, in Belize, 90–91
Moore, Harriet, 24
Multiplier effect, profit redistribution and, 33–34
Music, 111–12

National boundaries, 48
Nationalism, 49–54
National parks, 77
    in Kenya, 86
    nature tourism in, 76–77
Nation building, 17
Nation-states, impact of tourism on, 48–49
Native Americans, 17. *See also* Southwest; specific groups
    in Canada, 84
    casino gambling and, 39

cultures of, 97, 112, 113
    resentment of, 26
    space, tourism, and, 115
    travels of, 5–6
    women in Southwest, 25–26
Nature conservancy, 92
Nature tourism, 73–79
    ecotourism and, 84–90
    people and, 79–84
Navajo Indians, 115
Nepal, tourism employment in, 40–41
New Age tourism, 82
New Salem Historical Site (Illinois), 97–98
New tourism, ecotourism and, 88
Niches, 120
Non-English-speaking nations, language used in, 105
Non-Western societies, travel in, 5
Noritake, Kanzaki, 6
Nozama, Hiroko, 62

Oakes, Tim, 109–10
Opportunity costs, of tourism development, 34
Organizations, international, 43, 48

Pacific region, ethnic tourism in, 100
Panama, nature tourism and, 76
PCPD (popular, casual, passive, diversionary) ecotourism, 86
Pennsylvania, Amish in, 65–66, 102–3
People, as nature, 79–84
Pequot casino gambling, 39
Performance culture, 110–14
Picard, Michel, 100
Place, 114–18, 123–24
Planning, 42–45
Political behavior, 42–43
Political economy, tourism, society, and, 29–66
Politics, 42–43. See also Nationalism; Transnational dimensions of tourism
    of representation, 49–54
    of space and tourism, 115
Pollution, 69–70, 72

Populations, local, 23
Possum Point Biological Station, 91
Postmodern critique, 2
Pratt, Mary Louise, 60
Preservation, of natural environment, 75, 88
"Primitive peoples." See Indigenous peoples
Profits, repatriation of, 33
Prostitution, 62–63
Protest strategy, 57
Pueblo Indians, 26, 120

Railroads, southwestern tourism and, 24–25
Ranger, Terence, 97
Ranthamhor National Park (India), 76
Reason, tourism and, 15, 94–95
Recreational activities, 16
    pollution through, 69–70
Registers, of tourism, 107
Religion
    tourism as analogous with symbolism, 20
    as travel motive, 15
Repatriation of profits (leakage), 33
Representation, politics of, 49–54
Reserves, 77
    natural, 75–76
Resistance, to tourism, 55
Resorts, 13
Retreat
    from tourism, 55
    tourism as, 15
Reverse multipliers, 34
Revitalization, through tourism, 55
Richter, Linda, 48
Ritual, modern tourism and, 20
Ritzer, George, 19, 21
Rodriguez, Sylvia, 26
Rural tourism
    in Amish Pennsylvania, 65–66
    in Japan, 116–17
    in Tirol region, 63–66
Rwanda, nature tourism in, 76

Sacrilization, 20
Sani people (China), 103

Santa Elena Rainforest project, 87, 92

Santa Fe Railroad, Harvey and, 24, 25

Scotland, 116
 Isle of Skye and, 53–54

Seas, 78

Segmentation, of tourism industry, 84

Seiler-Baldinger, Annemarie, 113

"Service workers," prostitutes as, 63

Settlement, adaptation and, 4

Sexuality. *See also* Gender
 related to travel and tourism, 60, 62, 106

Sherpas, 40–41, 54

Shuji, Takasina, 7

Sindiga, Isaac, 54–55

Slash-and-burn beach tourism, 78

Smith, Valene, 2, 21, 80

Social class. *See* Classes

Social consequences of tourism, 54–59

Socialization of tourists, language and, 106

Social justice, 88–89

Society
 responses to tourism, 55–56
 tourism, political economy, and, 29–66

Southeast Asia, 49

Southwest, case study of touring, 23–27

Souvenirs, 112–13

Spaces, 114–18

Spain, Basques and, 95–96

Sports, 16

Sukimvit area (Bangkok, Thailand), 37

Sustainability, 85, 88–89

Swain, Margaret Bryne, 103

Sweet, Jill, 26, 113

Taiwan, 50

Taos Pueblo, 26

Technology, 88
 connections via, 121–22

Terminals, in airports, 1–2

Terrorism, 43

Thailand, 49, 70, 100–102
 indigenous tourism and, 82
 material culture in, 111, 113
 prostitution in, 62–63
 women in tourism and, 62

Third World. *See also* specific countries and regions
 tourism and economic development in, 36

Tirol region, rural tourism case study in, 63–66

Toledo Ecotourism Project, 91

Tourism. *See also* Travel; specific issues
 anthropological interest in, 2
 assumptions about, 11–12
 coping strategies for, 56–57
 development of, 31
 economic dependence upon, 119
 and economic development, 32–36
 eroticization of, 62
 globalization of, 118–21
 as mediated activity, 30
 modern, 12–17
 policies and plans, 42–45
 responses to, 55–56
 social consequences of, 54–59
 society, political economy, and, 29–66
 in space and place, 114–18
 transnational dimensions of, 45–49
 as work, 40–42

Tourism development, 119

Tourism industry, 12–17
 tourist as subject of, 18–23

Tourists, typology of, 21

Towner, John, 8–10

Transnational dimensions of tourism, 45–49. *See also* Globalization of tourism

Transportation, 13, 17, 24

Travel. *See also* Tourism
 concept of, 2
 historical perspective on, 4–12
 national limitations on, 46–47
 origins of term, 16
 rationales for, 15

Travel agencies, 13
Turner, Edith, 20
Turner, Victor, 20, 21
Twain, Mark, 17

United Nations, 43
United States, 44, 117
Urry, John, tourist typology of, 22

Vacations, 17

Waldren, Jacqueline, 22
Ward, G. K., 87
Ward, Martha, 63–66
Waswahili people, 55
Wealth, 5, 30–31, 37–38
Wearing, Stephen, 87
Weaver, David, 86
West, 4–5, 6, 7, 17
    female travel and, 60
    language of tourism and, 108
    leisure link in, 7
Whales
    hunting, 72
    watching, 86
Wildlife, 71–73
Women
    in Belize, 92
    in Japan, 62, 117–18
    Native American, 25–26
    in southwestern tourism, 25
Wood, R. C., 11, 100
Work, tourism as, 40–42
World Bank, 43
World systems, 118
World Tourism Organization, 37, 38,
    43, 85
World Wildlife Fund, 77, 92

Yao people, 101
Youth, tourism and, 121

Zeigler, Arlette, 103
Zerubavel, Yael, 50
Zukin, Sharon, 114–15, 119